KNOWLEDGE@WHARTON
ON BUILDING CORPORATE VALUE

KNOWLEDGE@WHARTON
On Building Corporate Value

MUKUL PANDYA, HARBIR SINGH,
ROBERT E. MITTELSTAEDT, JR.,
AND ERIC CLEMONS

John Wiley & Sons, Inc.

Library of Congress Cataloging-in-Publication Data:

Knowledge@Wharton on building corporate value / Mukul Pandya ... [et al.].
    p. cm.
  Includes bibliographical references and index.
  ISBN 0-471-00830-3 (CLOTH : alk. paper)
    1. Industrial management—Computer network resources. 2. Business enterprises—Computer network resources. 3. Electronic commerce. 4. Corporation—Valuation. I. Pandya, Mukul, 1957- II. Knowledge@Wharton.
  HD30.37 .K58 2002
  658.8'4—dc21

                                                 2002010163

Printed in the United States of America.
10 9 8 7 6 5 4 3 2 1

Contents

Part Two: Experience

INTRODUCTION

You Cannot Violate the Laws of Economics

Almost everyone knows the parable of the talents. The story describes a rich man who goes out of town after giving his servants five talent coins, two coins, and one coin each. When the master returns, he learns that while the servants who had five and two talents have doubled their money through business, the one with the single talent has simply buried it in the ground and done nothing. The furious master berates the servant, takes away the coin, and gives it to the one who has 10.

This deceptively simple story, which has been taught to children around the world for centuries, undoubtedly has deep philosophical connotations. But at its core also is a timeless message about value. The purpose of economic activity, the story implies, is to build value—and those who recognize that reality and act upon it are rewarded, while those who fail to do so are punished.

In 2002, as the aftershocks of the Enron debacle ripple through a weak economy, that message about building—and destroying—value seems particularly appropriate. In its heyday, Enron—the Houston-based energy giant—appeared to be a colossus that had revolutionized the way markets traded (and even thought about) energy and deserved its vaunted position in the top 10 of the *Fortune 500* list. As has increasingly become clear, that appearance was a sham; and thousands of Enron investors, employees, and others will have to pay the price for one of the biggest corporate bankruptcies in U.S. history. It is hard to imagine another case where more shareholder value was demolished—and so fast. (In hindsight, the Enron logo seems ominously apt. Someone should have asked earlier why it stood precariously on its edge, poised to topple over.) The consequences do not end with Enron. Arthur Andersen, Worldcom, Tyco International, Qwest Communications . . . the list goes on and on.

Even before these financial shenanigans hit the media spotlight, the effects of the Internet boom and bust were being felt across the United States—and to a more limited extent, the global—economy. For most of the late 1990s, the Internet was hailed as a revolutionary force that would transform everything. It was the age of the New Economy, when Old Economy rules and economics ceased to matter. Venture capital poured into Internet start-ups, investment bankers on Wall Street vied to take dot-com upstarts public, CEOs with strange names and ponytails pontificated from TV screens, and the NASDAQ stock index seemed to be heading for the stratosphere.

After Spring 2000, when it became clear that the hysteria could no longer be sustained and that the speculative bubble surrounding the Internet was about to burst, the pendulum began to swing in the other direction. The same companies that once set up separate dot-com units within their enterprises and bragged about how they "got" the working of the New Economy, now began to describe the Internet phenomenon as a mere speculative bubble. Now that it had burst, they argued, it was time to get back to business as usual.

Their refrain changed from "everything is different" to "nothing is different."

Knowledge@Wharton, the online research and business analysis journal of the Wharton School of the University of Pennsylvania, was launched in May 1999 when dot-com mania was going strong. During the past three years and more, the publication has witnessed —and covered—Internet entrepreneurs who claimed to be taking over the world as well as the collapse of their dot-com visions (accompanied, in some cases, by massive financial losses and in others by the acquisition of large personal fortunes). At the same time, *Knowledge@Wharton* profiled how the Internet was transforming the way established companies were doing business as they integrated the web into their operations. It often appeared that the main beneficiaries of the Internet's phenomenal growth were not the dot-coms, but large, established companies that were using the web to do things they could not do before.

From that vantage point, it became clear that both the extreme positions regarding the Internet—that it is a revolutionary force that will change the world immediately and that the dot-com phenomenon was just a speculative mania intended to con the gullible —were wrong. The truth lies in the middle: The Internet can be a powerful tool if companies and consumers learn how to use it creatively and imaginatively. When it is used right, the web enables companies to extend the impact of their own operations in dramatic ways. It opens up opportunities and possibilities that would either not have existed—or existed in a very limited way—before the Internet became a popular technology. Most importantly, the Internet makes it possible for companies to formulate information-based strategies that are rooted in economic sense and that can help them, in some instances, gain an edge over rivals. And when a company's strategy gives it a sustainable competitive advantage, that is when it is best positioned to build corporate value.

Exploring how companies can do just that—formulate information-based strategies that yield a sustainable competitive advantage—forms the theme of this book. Before doing that, however, it might be helpful to ask a question that is so basic that it is often forgotten and it has to be learned over and over again. The question is, "What is value?"

Economists have long distinguished between two notions of value for commodities: use value (or utility) and exchange value, or the rate at which commodities can be exchanged for one another (or for money). The focus of this book, however, is not the value of commodities but rather corporate value—which is measured by yardsticks such as profits and share prices. The purpose of corporate strategy is to enhance corporate value and shareholder wealth. In his book *Contemporary Strategy Analysis*, Robert M. Grant points out that strategy is a quest for profit. "Business is about creating value," he writes. "Value can be created in two ways: By production and by commerce." He explains that while production creates value by transforming objects (turning clay into pottery), commerce creates value not by transforming objects but by repositioning them in space and time, such as moving them from places where they are valued less to those where they are valued more.[1]

The Internet—and the information revolution that it has unleashed—does not change these rules of value any more than the invention of the steam engine or electricity did. It does, however, create new opportunities for value generation that did not exist before. For example, before the Internet became a popular force, the only "commerce" possible with used household objects might have been to sell them at a yard sale. The arrival of eBay—the online auction firm—has not only exponentially increased the size of that market to millions of potential buyers, but it also has enhanced opportunities for enhancing value. When hundreds of buyers bid against one another to buy an item on eBay, it adds more value to those objects than if their only outlet were a yard sale. Similarly, the existence of hundreds of sellers ensures that buyers, at least in most cases, do not get gouged. Little wonder that eBay's user base has grown to more than 42 million. The eBay model works because it helps buyers and sellers find one another in ways that would have been impossible before the Internet came along.[2]

This book, in many ways, explores how companies can build value through the Internet—and information-based strategies—just as countless individuals do every day through their transactions on eBay. It performs this task at two levels.

The first part of the book—the framework—offers theoretical tools and concepts that executives can use to examine how the Internet and the information revolution have transformed the global business scene. The initial chapters explore the key sources of competitive advantage and how success depends upon the ways in which companies position themselves in their industry, how they leverage their own capabilities and those of their alliance partners, and how effectively they neutralize their competition through their understanding of the competitive dynamic of their markets. The framework section also explains three important consequences of the Internet: the information effect, the brokerage effect, and the integration effect, and what these mean for companies. Furthermore, the book examines how the Internet affects customer behavior and the implications for companies. The Internet and the information revolution, in addition to creating new opportunities, also has created new risks. The final chapter in the framework section examines these risks and how companies can manage them.

Part Two of the book goes beyond the theoretical tools to the experiences of companies that have succeeded—and failed—in their experiments with the Internet and information-based strategies. The book looks at efforts in industries such as financial services and the media as well as the postage business. The final chapter in this section looks at what is living and what is dead in the world of *business-to-business* (B2B) e-commerce and online exchanges.

If one overarching lesson emerges from the pages that follow, it is that you cannot violate the laws of economics. The difference between the successes and the failures is that economic sense ultimately prevails, no matter what happens in the short run. Especially when we consider the use of technology to enable business, economics goes beyond dollars and is defined broadly to mean all the things that individuals (and businesses acting through individuals) trade off when making decisions. Money, time, convenience, service, reputation, and quality are all variables that enter the equation.

But we have said enough. It is time to begin this exploration. Because food and drink are primary to survival, that is where our journey begins: We look at lessons that two companies, Webvan and Tesco, learned (or failed to learn) as they tried to apply the Internet to the grocery business. Bon voyage.

ONE

Framework

1

I nspiration came to Louis H. Borders back in 1997. The cofounder of the Borders bookstore chain was reportedly opening a package of Japanese spices and specialty foods that he had ordered from a catalog when he realized that Internet-based commerce would never take off until someone figured out a way to deliver products to people's homes simply and inexpensively.[3] Determined to do just that, Borders came up with the concept for Webvan, an Internet venture whose ambitious goal was to revolutionize the low-margin, intensely competitive grocery business.

Armed with more than $122 million in initial funding from blue-chip companies such as CBS and Knight-Ridder and backing from top-notch Silicon Valley venture capital firms such as Benchmark Capital, Sequoia Capital, and Softbank, Borders and his associates declared Webvan open for business in the San Francisco Bay area on June 2, 1999. "Webvan Group today set a new standard for Internet retailing," the company declared in its press release.

Borders, then the CEO—who was later replaced by George Shaheen, the former boss of Andersen Consulting (now Accenture) —enthusiastically said, "Webvan fundamentally transforms and simplifies the way customers shop for their groceries."

As everyone now knows, for all its hubris Webvan turned out to be one of the Internet's most spectacular failures. After burning its way through more than $1.2 billion in two years after its high-profile launch, the company declared bankruptcy in July 2000. Most of its 2,000 employees were let go with minimal notice. Since then, the company has been liquidating its assets. Borders, through one of his companies, has petitioned the bankruptcy court to let him buy Webvan's software technology platform for $2.5 million and the assumption of $500,000 in debt.[4]

Does Webvan's Icarian flameout mean that the shoppers will never buy fruits and vegetables unless they can touch and smell them in a real-world store and that the online grocery business has no future? For part of the answer, look across the Atlantic Ocean to Britain's biggest retailer, Tesco, which traditionally operated a chain of supermarkets but has lately entered nonfood businesses, such as personal finance. The company's online arm, Tesco.com, was on track to garner $420 million in revenues in 2001, and analysts estimate its profits from the grocery business to be around $22 million.[5] Tesco.com is said to have nearly one million registered users, 840,000 orders a year, and is expanding into categories such as baby products and wine. Tesco.com claims that it has become "the largest and most successful Internet-based grocery home shopping service in the world."[6]

On the surface, Webvan and Tesco had the same goal: both companies wanted to harness the power of the Web to deliver groceries to shoppers. That, however, is where the similarity ended. Anyone who compares Webvan's approach to the online grocery business with Tesco's will see that each company pursued a strategy that was not just different from the other's but poles apart. For example, while Webvan made huge bets on the Internet's ability to change shoppers' behaviors, Tesco made tiny ones. Webvan wanted to overthrow the grocery industry's infrastructure and replace it with its own, while Tesco used the industry's infrastructure to keep costs low. Webvan spent enormous sums of cash trying to build a brand and a customer base while Tesco used its existing brand and customers to drive its online business. (Of course, it is also true that Tesco began with some crucial advantages vis-à-vis Webvan. Webvan had to build name and scale *de novo*, while Tesco could leverage both. In addition, Webvan made its investments in the United States, where grocery shopping offers low margins to sellers, while Tesco began in Britain, where margins are significantly higher than they are in the United States.)

Jerry Wind, a Wharton professor of marketing who explores the actions of both companies in a book titled *Convergence Marketing*, notes that Webvan started with the notion that it would have to do everything from scratch and that a new type of firm would be required to do it. "But the company did not take into account the logistics issues that were involved," he says. "As such, Webvan had to create a whole logistics company. In contrast, Tesco followed a simple strategy. From the beginning, it saw Tesco.com as one more channel through which to reach its existing customers as well as some new ones. It tried to provide a multi-channel experience to the customers that it had already attracted."[7] That strategy allowed Tesco.com's online grocery business to thrive.

It might be worthwhile examining the strategies of Webvan and Tesco in greater detail to show how those differences led to different results.

Webvan: Speed Kills

From the beginning, an ambitious winner-take-all attitude marked Webvan's approach to selling groceries online. In the late spring of 1999, just as Webvan was getting ready to launch its Web site, Borders told *The Wall Street Journal* that Webvan planned to sell $300 million worth of groceries a year from a single warehouse in Oakland, California. "If it thrives, and even if it does not, Mr. Borders plans to open another enormous grocery warehouse in Atlanta a few months later. Down the road are plans for at least 20 more such facilities throughout the United States in practically every city big enough to support a major-league sports team," *The Wall Street Journal* wrote.[8]

Borders raised an initial $120 million in venture capital and spent a significant part of it building the state-of-the-art warehouse, "a 330,000-square-foot behemoth adorned with five miles of conveyor belts and $3 million of electrical wiring," according to *The Wall Street Journal*. Although other online grocers such as Peapod were in trouble, Webvan had high hopes that it would be able to succeed where others had failed because it had invested heavily in high-tech infrastructure. Webvan executives believed that this investment would translate into much higher productivity and that this strategy would enable the company not only to beat out other online grocers but also traditional brick-and-mortar supermarkets.

Unlike shoppers in traditional grocery stores who moved around aisles with carts, Webvan workers would stand at automated carousels equipped with nearly 9,000 products. Thanks to its unique technology, Webvan executives predicted, its workers would be 10 times as productive as traditional shoppers—and this scenario would translate into faster profitability. Borders claimed that the Oakland warehouse would be profitable in six to 12 months while other warehouses might break even in as little as 60 days. "I do not see any reason why an Internet company should take five to 10 years to be profitable," Borders argued.[9]

If higher worker productivity was one key element of Webvan's strategy, another was its assumption that time-starved shoppers would respond overwhelmingly to the convenience of being able to order products on Webvan's Web site 24 hours a day and have them home-delivered within a 30-minute window of their choosing. This goal, the company said, would be accomplished by having a fleet of customized delivery vans to handle distribution. So efficient would this process be, Webvan believed, that customers would be able to shop at Webvan at the same or lower prices as they did at traditional grocery stores. "Prices are up to 5 percent less on average than typical supermarkets, and delivery is free for orders of $50 or more," the company said.[10]

Based on these twin assumptions of super-efficient worker productivity and customer-friendly delivery, Webvan embarked upon aggressive growth after its Web site was launched. By July 1999, the company announced that it had hired the Bechtel Group, an engineering firm in San Francisco, to build 26 highly automated warehouses for $1 billion. Each warehouse was to be modeled on the facility in Oakland. Webvan clearly wanted to grow—and fast. (A note of caution is in order: The desire for massive investments in scale per se is not necessarily a recipe for failure. In fact, in the drug wholesaling business, companies made massive investments to support efficient warehousing operations and customer-friendly distribution, and the only survivors in that industry are companies that ramped up their scale rapidly. Webvan, however, chose this approach in the grocery business, where profit margins are minuscule, and the willingness of customers to adopt online grocery shopping in large enough volumes to support the investments in scale was uncertain.)

Two factors contributed to Webvan's aggressive drive for growth. The first was the threat of emerging competition. Peapod, with sales of some $40 million, had a head start over Webvan in the online grocery market, but it was bleeding cash. A greater challenge seemed to stem from HomeGrocer, a Seattle-based online grocery firm. At around the same time that Webvan launched its operations, Amazon.com announced that it had bought a stake in HomeGrocer. The Amazon-HomeGrocer combination could have affected Webvan's prospects significantly. For Webvan, the way to head off that threat seemed to lie in making a run for dominance.

Webvan executives believed that the threat of competition made the company's drive for market dominance necessary. The second factor—easy availability of capital—made that drive possible.

In 1999, capital was flowing in tidal waves towards technology and Internet companies, especially those backed by leading Silicon Valley venture capitalists such as Benchmark Capital and Sequoia Capital—both of which were solidly in Webvan's corner. That year, venture-capital investments reached an all-time high of $48.3 billion, an increase of more than 150 percent over 1998's total, according to the NVCA and Venture Economics. More than 90 percent of that capital went to high-tech and Web-based companies.[11] Before a company could qualify to grab a piece of that action, however, it had to convince potential investors that it was willing to live by the Internet economy's unwritten rule of growing at breakneck speed.

Even if someone at Webvan had wanted to first try out its online grocery model in one city, improve upon it, and then expand to other cities, the financial climate of those times would have had little patience with that approach. Many people involved with Internet startups believed that they had a narrow window of opportunity and that they had to act fast before it slammed shut. In an interview with *The New York Times*, David Beirne, a venture capitalist with Benchmark Partners and an early backer of Webvan, described the situation as a catch-22. "We had a unique opportunity to raise a lot of capital and build a business faster than Sam Walton rolled out Wal-Mart," he said. "But in order to raise the money, we had to promise investors rapid growth."[12]

If rapid growth was what Webvan's investors wanted, that is what they got. The company began rolling out massive warehouses at a cost of more than $30 million per warehouse in areas such as Suwanee, Georgia (serving the Atlanta market) and Carol Stream, Illinois (serving the Chicago area). Smaller distribution centers were set up in areas such as Los Angeles and San Diego, among others. On November 5, 1999, with hardly a few months of online product sales under its belt, Webvan went public in a stock offering co-underwritten by some of Wall Street's most blue-blooded investment banks: Goldman Sachs, Merrill Lynch, BancBoston Robertson Stephens, Bear Stearns & Co., and Salomon Smith Barney. Webvan sold 25 million shares priced at $15 each, but so heady was the buzz surrounding its IPO that the stock soared to a short-lived high of $34 on its first day of trading, giving Webvan a market capitalization of $7.6 billion.

Over the next year and a half, Borders and other Webvan executives strove mightily to remain true to their vision for the company. Among its most ambitious moves was to recruit George Shaheen, the CEO of Andersen Consulting, as Webvan's CEO, with Borders taking the chairman's post. As the months passed, however, it became clear that Webvan was unable to get away from one simple fact: Webvan was spending more money on acquiring customers and products and that it could make by selling them. Some analysts estimate that Webvan lost more than $130 per order, including depreciation, marketing, and other overhead.[13]

In an attempt to gain economies of scale, which might have led to profitability, Webvan in September 2000 merged with its erstwhile rival HomeGrocer, but that, too, could not postpone the decline. In documents filed with the *Securities and Exchange Commission* (SEC), Webvan reported that in the fiscal year ending December 31, 2000, the company had lost $453 million on sales of $178 million.[12] By April 2001, Shaheen had left Webvan, and the company was scaling back dramatically. This change included dropping plans for the construction of new warehouses as well as slashing marketing expenses. Lowering marketing costs immediately hurt sales. Even more significantly, though, these actions added to the perception that Webvan was in trouble and that it was unable to stanch its financial hemorrhage.

Goldman Sachs, meanwhile, was making intense efforts to find a buyer or new investors for Webvan. When these efforts failed, Webvan had little choice but to announce on July 9, 2001 that it was closing its operations and would declare bankruptcy.

How Flawed Assumptions Misled Webvan

In retrospect, what did Webvan do wrong? The company's assumptions led directly to its blunders. To recount, Webvan assumed the following:

1. That a very large number of people would prefer to buy groceries online and have them delivered at home, rather than buying them at a physical supermarket. This belief led them

to reckon that Webvan's sales would explode and that people would place a high value on not having to go to a physical supermarket.

2. That so much inefficiency existed in the grocery industry's infrastructure that Webvan would garner a bigger margin if it rebuilt the whole infrastructure by doing all its own warehousing and logistics and moving further up the value chain by cutting out the wholesalers

3. That if a Web site gave shoppers more choice and a wider selection of products, that people would be willing to pay at least the same price (if not a premium) for the privilege of shopping online as they did in a physical store

As time was to show, each of these assumptions was wrong. Webvan's biggest mistake was assuming that people did not want to shop in a supermarket. Large numbers of shoppers have not made their purchase decisions before going to the store. This situation is where Webvan ignored the basic laws of economics: The company could not get people to buy something they did not need. When it comes to groceries, a supermarket cannot get shoppers to buy a delivery service that is convenient for them if they have not decided what to order.

Had Webvan made its groceries dramatically cheaper—selling them, say, at half price—then conceivably some people would have thought more about their needs and organized their shopping behavior to make the process work. But if the groceries are the same price online as they are in the stores, it does not have the same incentive except for a very small percentage of the population that finds buying online more convenient.

Webvan's second mistake was to try to reinvent the entire infrastructure that the grocery industry has evolved over the past 100 years. It turns out that the infrastructure might be more efficient than people realize. Webvan spent huge amounts trying to integrate this infrastructure, and it also did not do it as efficiently as it thought it would. It would have taken years for Webvan to learn how to integrate its infrastructure, and it ran out of capital long before that.

Webvan's third mistake was to choose San Francisco as its starting point. The company assumed that this market had people with high incomes and a higher interest in the quality of food, and its executives thought that this place would be good to start, but that market is very difficult from a traffic standpoint. San Francisco has hills and houses that are hard to reach, and these factors make it a nightmarish location for companies that have to deliver things. That added to Webvan's implementation problems.

If all these errors are added together, the result is that Webvan invested $1 billion based on very shaky assumptions that do not hold up under economic scrutiny. An electric company that wanted to invest $1 billion in building a new power station would have to look long and hard at the demand for electricity before making a decision. A chemical company would have to look thoroughly at the demand for plastics before deciding to build a billion-dollar plastics plant.

Webvan, however, did not go through that exercise. So rosy was the view inside the dot-com bubble that it did not need to—and the company and its investors eventually paid the price for that mindset.

Tesco: Slow and Steady

With $32 billion in annual sales, Tesco bills itself as the "number one food retailer in the U.K. and the largest e-grocer in the world."[14] When it wanted to enter the world of e-business, however, its approach was dramatically different than Webvan's. Tesco executives recently told *Business Week* that back in 1996, the company tested whether shoppers were willing to buy groceries online by introducing a single Web site at one store in Osterley, England. In fact, as *Business Week* notes, "Tesco's big bet was to bet small."[14]

Early in its e-business experiment, Tesco realized that it would have to address one key issue: should it supply shoppers with groceries taken off the shelves of its existing stores, or would demand be so high as to require the construction of dedicated warehouses? Tesco decided not to invest in the construction of special warehouses until it had a better sense of online consumer demand. The company kept testing and readjusting its online sales process, letting customers order groceries on the Internet and supplying them from its existing stores, for nearly two years—which was not only an extremely long period in "Internet time" but also coincided with the height of the dot-com boom.

At the time, Tesco was often criticized as a company that did not "get it" and that stood timidly by letting other, so-called "purer" Web-based retailers forge ahead. By plodding along at its tortoise-like pace, however, Tesco learned a lesson that its hare-like rivals did not—that for the time being, online grocery shopping represented a niche trend rather than a full-blown mass market. By 2000, for example, although Tesco.com's annualized online sales were running at a rate of $420 million a year, this figure was less than 2 percent of the company's total revenues of $32 billion.

Taking the gradual approach helped Tesco.com learn at least two significant lessons. First, rather than promising ambitious home deliveries, the company experimented with having customers order their groceries online but pick them up at a store near their home. Customers saved on the time and effort that it took to pick products

off the shelf, and they found that they had a bag of groceries wait-
ing for them when they arrived at the store. At the same time, however, if they wanted to add one or two items to their order, they had
the option to do so.

In addition to prepackaging orders for shoppers, Tesco.com also
began to deliver groceries to customers' homes near each store. In
an important departure from Webvan's strategy, however, the company imposed a delivery charge right from the beginning. Not only
did this approach help Tesco.com recover part of its delivery costs,
but it also had another positive result: the company saw the shoppers' order sizes increase as households endeavored to get maximum mileage for the delivery charge.

This approach has kept Tesco.com growing. On September 18,
2001, Terry Leahy, chief executive of Tesco, PLC, announced that
in 2001 Tesco.com's sales were "up 77 percent on last year, a period
when we were still rolling out the service. Grocery home shopping
made good profits, however overall Tesco.com made a small loss of
£3 million (in the first half, reflecting the launch cost of new sites
such as our wine warehouse." He added that Tesco.com "made
excellent progress and we now reach 94 percent of the U.K. population. In the first half our grocery home shopping operation achieved
like for like sales of nearly 40 percent and created 600 new jobs."

In an effort to extend its model to the United States, in June
2000 Tesco.com announced a partnership with Safeway, one of the
largest food and drug retailers in the United States. The company,
which is slightly bigger than Tesco—its annual revenues are $32
billion—operates more than 1,700 supermarkets in the United
States and Canada. Since January 2000, Safeway had been providing online grocery shopping through a Texas-based unit called
GroceryWorks. As part of the deal, Tesco.com bought a 35 percent

stake in GroceryWorks for an investment of $22 million in cash as well as intellectual property and technical resources, while Safeway held 50 percent of GroceryWorks. According to Leahy, the objective was to introduce the Tesco.com model to American grocery shoppers in collaboration with Safeway. "With Tesco's know how and the Safeway brand, we have the perfect combination to bring grocery home shopping to the world's largest market," Leahy said.[15]

Will Tesco.com's approach work in a market where Webvan failed? It well could. The reason is because Tesco used technology to make the existing shopping process—that people were used to—more efficient rather than trying to totally reinvent a process with which people were not familiar.

Tesco is hardly the only British retailer trying out this approach. Another leading supermarket chain, Waitrose, which operates 135 stores around Britain, has introduced a system called Waitrose@Work in which the company delivers groceries to offices. To sign up its workers for the program, companies must have at least 500 employees and register with the supermarket company. Waitrose also provides home deliveries of groceries in selected markets in Britain.

Neither Tesco nor Waitrose tried to reinvent the whole infrastructure of the grocery industry. They did not incur a large capital cost. They just used the Internet to increase the efficiency of a piece of their business.

Wind sees considerable potential in Tesco's approach. He says that Tesco "basically has to worry just about distribution from the store to the home. This is a far more economical model—and it offers the opportunity for considerable cross-selling. Tesco has found out that by adopting this model, its online customers have increased their purchases from the stores, and people who used to

Table 1.1   Two Approaches to Selling Groceries Online

	Webvan	*Tesco*
Timing	Rapid rollout	Gradual rollout
Scale	Large	Incremental
Key value drivers	Reinvent infrastructure	Modify infrastructure
	Create new brand identity	Leverage existing brand identity
Outcome	Bankruptcy	Profitability

shop in the stores have increased their shopping on the Web. So there is a crossover effect between the two channels."

This model is also starting to catch on in other parts of the world. Caprabo, a European supermarket chain that is "replicating the Tesco model in Spain, has announced that it expects to break even this year—in less than a year," Wind says. "The reason is simple: The entire cost of launching Caprabo.com was as much as opening a 20,000-square-foot store. And the volume of sales has been amazing. Within the first three months, even though it was just one store out of a network of 52 stores that introduced online sales, that one store already accounts for 6 percent of Caprabo's total sales volume."[16]

With 20-20 hindsight, some critics have blamed Webvan's failure on the arrogance of its executives. This view, however, is oversimplified. When an organization gets as seriously lost as Webvan did, it is not enough to do soul searching about the errors of its leaders. It is time to start thinking seriously about strategy.

2

Creating Internet Strategies
for Competitive Advantage

I n the fall of 1998, a consultant from a Big Five professional services firm was speaking at a conference in Philadelphia, and he
told his audience a memorable anecdote. Two students approached
a venture capitalist with a concept for a dot-com company.
Intrigued by what he heard in the first few minutes of the students'
pitch, the venture capitalist asked whether they had a business
plan. The students flourished a document—all of three handwritten
pages—and the venture capitalist was sold. A handshake later, he
promised cash. Soon, the capital was delivered, and a dot-com was
born. It was a deal typical of those times.

Today, the fate of that company is unknown, but if its track
record is anything like that of many Internet startups, it is probably
dismal. For much of 2000 and 2001, dot-coms that were regarded
as revolutionaries that would someday conquer the world have
been fading from the scene. Webvan might have been one of the
biggest disasters in dot-com land, but it is hardly the only one.
Other notable flops include business-to-consumer companies such

as eToys and Pets.com as well as Internet access providers such as PSI Net and Exodus Communications. Webmergers, a San Francisco-based firm, estimates that 806 Internet companies around the world have shut down since January 2000. Of that number, "at least 537 Internet companies shut down or declared bankruptcy in 2001 alone, more than twice as many as in the previous year, when 225 dot-coms failed," it noted.[1]

As the survivors have discovered only too well, the Internet is serious business meant for companies that appreciate the laws of economics. And increasingly, those companies appear to include large, so-called brick-and-mortar companies rather than the dot-com upstarts that were riding high at the peak of the Internet bubble.

For companies eager to approach their Internet ventures like real businesses—in other words, with real revenues and the prospect of someday turning profits—it is important to consider a conceptual framework to analyze Internet strategies. In addition, it is crucial to examine business models and examine their components and also look into what makes some business models better than others at providing a competitive edge to companies that adopt them.

The commercial deployment of the Internet was accompanied by the availability of enormous amounts of venture capital to finance dot-com ventures, as is evident from Webvan's experience described in the previous chapter. According to a Wharton research paper[2], "United States venture capital investment in 1995 was only $520 million. This figure grew to $31.9 billion in 1999."

Three Effects

What was it about the Internet, however, that prompted normally hard-nosed venture capitalists to open their wallets to fund entre-

Table 2.1   Framework: Using Information-Based Technology
for Competitive Advantage

	Concept	Example
Three Effects	Communication	Google
	Brokerage	eBay
	Integration	Covisint
Sources	Positioning	Defense firms
	Creating/leveraging capabilities	Coca-Cola
	Neutralizing competition	Price warfare
Business models	Novelty	Autobytel.com
	Efficiency	Amazon.com
	Complementarities	Expedia.com
	Lock-in	Hotmail

preneurial ventures to such an unprecedented degree? Part of the reason was because they recognized that Internet technology has three broad effects. First, it has a communication effect, which means that it dramatically reduces the cost of finding and transferring information. Second, it has a brokerage effect—the Web makes it easy to connect buyers and sellers. And third, it has an integration effect, which is to say that it transforms buyer-seller relationships and has an impact upon supply and value chains.

Anyone who has searched for information on a search engine like Google or Alta Vista can attest to the usefulness of the communication effect. The Internet has made it enormously easy to look for—and find—vast amounts of information, in addition to making it much less expensive to store and transmit it. The operative word, though, is *less* expensive—and not entirely free, as dot-com executives sometimes assumed. In their relentless drive to acquire readers —or "eyeballs," as Web traffic was notoriously described—that was a point that dot-com entrepreneurs often overlooked.

Take the *Encyclopedia Britannica*, for example. Some years ago, the hardbound paper tomes cost $1,600. During the Internet boom, after a bruising battle with its rival, Microsoft's Encarta, Britannica.com, the online arm of the encyclopedia publisher, experimented with giving away its content free and generating revenues through advertising. Traffic on the Web site quickly soared, making Britannica.com one of the most popular Internet destinations. By March 2001, however, Britannica.com recognized that it would be unable to sustain its free operations and started charging its readers a subscription fee of $50 a year or $7.95 a month.[3] "There was a time not along ago when most observers believed that Internet services had to be supported mainly through advertising," Britannica.com Chief Executive Don Yannias said in a statement. "We are out there in the marketplace, however, and we're convinced that a diversified business model combining free and subscription-supported products is the road to success."[4]

The Internet's brokerage effect is equally powerful. Some analysts compare the Web to a giant market marked by "openness, informality, and interactivity." This effect makes it possible for Internet users to access global markets at little extra cost, allowing small businesses to target the same customers as larger organizations. Jeff Bezos, CEO of Amazon.com, for example, has described his company's role as a broker that stands between buyers and sellers.

An even more dramatic example is eBay, the California-based auction site (www.eBay.com) that claims its mission is "to help practically anyone trade practically anything on Earth." Founded in September 1995, eBay in 2002 has more than 40 million registered users. "Today, eBay commands more than 80 percent of the online consumer and small-business auction market. It operates a customer friendly site featuring more than 126 million auction listings and

18,000 categories, twice as many as the previous year. It boasts annualized gross merchandise sales of nearly $11 billion."[5]

Finally, the Internet has an integration effect. The Internet realigns players in industry value chains as some are disintermediated as a result of the new technology. When the value chain changes, it provides an opportunity to create value. The Internet transforms industry value chains in significant ways. (A value chain is the sequence of activities involved in the transformation of inputs into outputs; it includes all the transactions performed before a product reaches the end consumer.) Because the Web makes it easy to search for information and also directly connects buyers and sellers, it can knock sections of middlemen out of the value chain by eliminating the need for their participation in transactions. A case in point is online stock offerings. In the past, those who wanted to buy stocks in an IPO had to deal with the investment bank managing the offering. On the Web, sites such as E*Offering.com— which was acquired by Wit Capital in May 2000 for $328 million— began to allow IPO issuers and buyers to deal directly with one another.[6]

Sometimes, the transformation of the value chain results in the emergence of new intermediaries stepping in to replace the old. These so-called infomediaries gain power through the Internet. The reason is because they can mine customer transaction data, making so-called mass customization possible. For example, some online stores recommend new books or CDs based on the past purchasing patterns of their customers.

Thus, the Internet creates entrepreneurial opportunities. How, though, should entrepreneurs exploit them? The answer depends in part upon the kind of business models that entrepreneurs develop to gain competitive advantage over their rivals.

References to "business models" are frequent when aspiring entrepreneurs pitch their plans to potential investors. While the popular media uses the term loosely and vaguely, it is crucial to attempt a precise definition: a business model is "a unique configuration of elements comprising the organization's goals, strategies, processes, technologies, and structure, conceived to create value for the customers and thus compete successfully in a particular market."[7] In other words, the business model is what enables a company to capture and deliver value to its customers.

Business models must have four important elements: scalability, complementary resources and capabilities, relation-specific assets, and knowledge-sharing routines:

1. **Scalability**: Information assets, which dominate the e-business world, have a unique property: they are generally costly to produce in the first place, but once produced they are very easy (and relatively inexpensive) to reproduce. In order to exploit this aspect of competitive advantage on the Web, it follows that companies must develop business models that are scalable.

2. **Complementary resources and capabilities**: A company that has an innovative business model can initially use its technological prowess to march over its competitors. Entrepreneurs would be wrong, however, to believe that this advantage is long lasting. In order to protect their competitive positions, companies that lead in the digital arena might have to acquire physical assets to keep their competitors at bay. An example is AOL's acquisition of Time Warner's brick-and-mortar assets, which might have been driven by this need. Still, no one should assume that these so-called conduit-content combinations gen-

erate value automatically. AOL Time Warner's difficulties in this regard were made dramatically clear in the summer of 2002 with the departure of Robert Pittman, the company's chief operating officer. As *The New York Times* pointed out in a report about the company's problems, "As the smoke lifts, it has become clear that the company that resulted from America Online's acquisition of Time Warner is very much like the old Time Warner."[8]

3. **Relation-specific assets:** No individual firm can hope to dominate the Internet, which is a complex network designed precisely to avoid such dominance. As a result, networks of alliances become increasingly important. Business models on the Web must recognize that competitive advantage in e-business is often based on managing collaborative relationships well with key partners.

4. **Knowledge-sharing routines:** This condition follows from the previous one, which emphasizes the need for strong, collaborative relationships. These relationships can only become truly effective if the collaborators develop mechanisms through which they can share knowledge with one another. Such knowledge sharing will help the partners enhance their collective competitive advantage over rivals and their partners.

From Business Models to Key Elements of Competitive Advantage

A company might come up with a creative business model that explores the Internet's information effect, brokerage effect, and integration effect. The business model, however, which spells out the value proposition that the company offers its customers, is only one of the factors that the company needs in order to gain and sustain a competitive advantage. It is helpful to view the key elements of competitive advantage as a triad consisting of three elements:

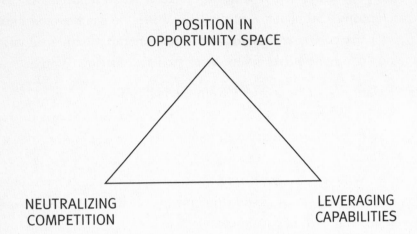

POSITION IN
OPPORTUNITY SPACE

NEUTRALIZING
COMPETITION

LEVERAGING
CAPABILITIES

A. Position in opportunity space

After the end of the Cold War, many former defense contractors had to scramble to change their positioning in their industries. No longer able to produce defense products, they had to find ways to adapt their technologies to commercial uses. After the terrorist attacks on September 11, 2001 and the onset of the Bush administration's war against terrorism, however, such companies are now exploring opportunities to reposition themselves as providers of security products.

As this example shows, if companies want to gain a competitive advantage over their rivals, they must position themselves appropriately. If they succeed, they can find themselves in attractive markets that offer lucrative profits.

Companies can strengthen their positioning in their industries in three ways:

1. **They need to identify barriers to entry.** Academic research shows that when entry into an industry is easy—because barriers to entry are low—profits in that industry are lower than in industries where entry is more difficult. This factor was clearly evident during the Internet boom and bust. During the early days of the dot-com boom, when a few online retailers began to provide e-commerce services, imitators jumped onto the bandwagon with great ease. In the pet food market, for example, companies such as Pets.com vied with rivals such as Petopia.com, Petjungle.com, Paw.net, and Petstore.com (among others) to establish leadership. That sort of free-for-all makes it very difficult for any company to position itself well. It just makes competition much more intense, in addition to often provoking price wars and depressing profits.

2. **They must identify attractive market segments.** An industry might be overcrowded, but an individual segment in that industry might see a rising demand. Companies that are positioned to sell those products in that industry tend to do well.

3. **Companies must understand the nature of the competitive game in their industry.** Different factors drive success or failure in different industries. In software, the nature of competition is determined by the development and control of industry standards. In steel, efficiency holds the key. In perfumes, brand image forms the basis for competition. Companies must understand not only the present

basis of the competitive game in their industry but also how it is changing and where it is headed in the future.

B. Leveraging capabilities

Capabilities have long been recognized as a key source of competitive advantage. The term "capability" refers to the combination of skills, resources, and knowledge that companies bring to the table when they compete. Companies differ not only in their capabilities but also in the ways in which they use their capabilities.

In order to gain competitive advantage, companies should aim to develop capabilities that are unique. A case in point is Coca-Cola, whose brand management and supply chain/sourcing capabilities are unique to the soft drink industry. Capabilities should also be difficult to replicate. In addition, the capabilities should be widely applicable so that they can be spread over several products and services and not just be one-trick ponies.

C. Neutralizing competition

As important as it is for companies to position themselves correctly and develop capabilities that set themselves apart, they should also adopt strategies that anticipate competitive reactions.

The outcomes of a strategy are often considerably different when competitive reactions are taken into account. For instance, suppose that a company cuts prices, expecting to gain more sales and profits. If competitors also respond by lowering profits, a price war could ensue, and the downward spiral could hurt everyone involved. Neutralizing competition also requires companies to be aware of their competitors' capabilities—and, increasingly, those of their allies.

Competitive Advantage and Business Value: Spilling the Beenz

Once a company has positioned itself appropriately by identifying its value proposition and most profitable segments, unleashed its capabilities, and figured out a business model that will leave its rivals far behind, it can then focus on building business value. To examine how that might—or might not—happen, consider the rise and fall of a company called Beenz.com, whose assets were taken over on October 4, 2001 by Carlson Marketing Group, a Minnesota-based relationship marketing company.

Beenz.com believed that it could mint money—or at least virtual money. The company, which was headquartered in New York City and also had operations in Europe and Asia, had the ambitious goal of launching a universal, Web-based currency called "beenz" that would work for online retailers, much like frequent-flier miles do for airlines. Customers earned beenz when they shopped at stores such as Barnesandnoble.com or MP3.com, and they could spend their beenz at some 300 Web sites around the world. Merchants, meanwhile, could redeem beenz for cash. Launched in March 1999, Beenz.com attracted high-profile investors such as Lawrence Ellison, CEO of Oracle, Vivendi, and Softbank. The company bragged that it had more than five million users who had performed more than 25 million beenz transactions. Although its competitors included rivals such as Flooz.com, Cybercash, and CyberGold—all of which are now defunct —Beenz.com seemed positioned to succeed as an online currency.

What was unusual about Beenz.com? Certainly, it was not the fact that it operated loyalty programs, which have been around much longer than the Internet. According to Raffi Amit, co-director of the Wharton E-Business Initiative, and Christoph Zott, a professor at INSEAD, it was the fact that the value that beenz.com created did not reside within the firm per se but rather in the network of partners that it brought together. In other words, beenz.com coordinated the activities of several partners to create value for its customers. "Without its partner vendors, Beenz.com would not create significant value," say Amit and Zott. "Its core product—the virtual currency beenz—does not have a high stand-alone value." And that, as we shall see next, is what played a key role in Beenz.com's downfall.

Amit and Zott argued that case in a paper titled "Value Drivers of E-Commerce Business Models," pointing out that the way companies construct business models is crucial to their ability to create value. Unless their strategy for doing so is appropriate—and based on the laws of economics—they could end up destroying value rather than creating it.

As part of their research, Amit and Zott constructed a framework called the eValue framework to help executives understand major value drivers of e-commerce. They note that "the value-creating potential of any business model is enhanced by the extent to which these factors are present."[9]

Understanding the value drivers of e-commerce business models could help companies stave off disaster. While various reasons account for the failure of dot-com companies, Amit believes that flawed business models were at the core of these companies' weaknesses. Had these companies focused on their true value drivers, their chances of success would have been enhanced—in part because their business models would have been more robust.

Amit and Zott point out that business models offer the "relevant perspective for understanding new business structures in the information age." Academic literature almost entirely ignores this approach. As a term, however, "business model" is often used ambiguously, with the result that contradictions and misconceptions abound about the concept. Amit and Zott attempt a precise definition. They describe a business model as "the architectural configuration of the components of transactions designed to exploit business opportunities." The revenue model, in contrast, refers to "the specific ways in which a business model enables revenue generation."

In other words, a business model depicts the architectural configuration of economic exchanges. It describes the ways in which a company enables transactions that create value for all participants, including partners, suppliers, and customers. So while a business model is about value creation, a revenue model centers on value appropriation. Revenues can be realized through a combination of subscription fees, advertising fees, transactional income (for example, fixed transactional fees, referral fees, and fixed/variable commissions) and more.

Amit and Zott offer a simple example to show the difference between a business model and a revenue model. For example, in the case of Beenz.com, the Web-currency company, the company "generates revenues by charging a higher price for the beenz that it sells to vendors than the price it pays for buying them back. Like a bank, it profits from a bid-ask spread on transactions," the researchers point out. The company's business model, however, is "that of a clearing house for a virtual currency with affiliated vendors." The company's revenue and business models are thus distinct, though they complement each other.

Having explained the architecture of business models, Amit and Zott go on to describe the main elements of their eValue framework, which they use to examine the value-creating potential of various business models. The four key value drivers, in their view, are efficiency, complementarities, lock-in, and novelty.

1. **Efficiency**: The Internet makes it possible to increase efficiency in several ways. One of the most significant is its ability to reduce so-called information asymmetries between buyers and sellers. Here is an example. If a customer is looking for a new car, in the traditional world he or she would have had to

suffer the tedium of going to dealership after dealership to get information about auto prices and availability. A Web site such as Autobytel.com, however, transforms this situation. It not only provides the potential car buyer with detailed, comparative information about different models, but it also "facilitates a reverse market, in which buyers put their desired purchase up for bid among vendors," say Amit and Zott. "The buying process is thereby substantially simplified and accelerated, and bargaining costs are reduced." A business model can unlock hidden value by enhancing transactional efficiencies by enabling reduced search costs, transaction speed, reduced distribution costs, reduced inventory costs, and more. Although arguably this goal has been the principal intention of all automation, the Internet and information-based strategies change the scale at which these transactional efficiencies can help generate value.

2. **Complementarities**: Companies have long known that they can leverage value creation for their own products when they bundle them with complementary products from other suppliers. On the Internet, bundling complementary products or services together is crucial because it can play a vital part in building online virtual communities. For example, when customers buy a plane ticket to a certain city on Expedia.com, an online travel site, they get an e-mail giving information about that city's weather, car rental agencies, hotels, restaurants, and so on. Such services "enhance the value of the core product and make it convenient for users to book travel and vacations with e-bookers," said Amit and Zott. In addition to exploiting complementarities among products and services, a business model enables value creation by capturing the benefits from combining online with offline businesses (such as www.officedepot.com), complemen-

tarities among technologies, and complementarities among the activities of participants in the business model.

3. **Lock-in:** This term refers to the capability of a business model to prompt users to engage in repeat transactions. Lock-in can be enabled, for example, by creating switching costs that customers would face if they were to switch to a different service provider. Switching costs are created through loyalty programs, by providing transaction safety and creating the perception of trust, through familiarity with the site, and also through customization and personalization. One example of a company that uses lock-in effectively is Amazon.com, which has developed an extremely simple "one-click ordering system" for customers who order books, videos, CDs, or other products. This ease of use—as well as the fact that Amazon's database has credit card information on file for its customers that can be used for transaction after transaction—locks in buyers who return for more purchases. Another instance of an effective lock-in strategy is Hotmail, the e-mail service that now belongs to Microsoft. Hotmail grew rapidly by offering free e-mail service to clients. Once these customers had signed up to receive their e-mail through Hotmail, the inconvenience of having to change e-mail addresses represented the switching cost that kept them loyal even after other providers began offering free e-mail.

4. **Novelty:** Innovation has always involved the introduction of novel products or services or processes. The Internet, however, offers even more possibilities to innovate in the manner in which transactions are enabled—by introducing new business and revenue models. eBay, the first firm to introduce customer-to-customer auctions, enables even low-value items to be traded online. And Autobytel.com, which transformed the car-buying process in the United States, links potential buyers, auto dealers,

finance companies, and insurance companies. Amit and Zott believe that "by identifying and incorporating valuable new complementary products and services, combining activities, and integrating technologies into their business models in novel ways," these companies were capable of tapping into new sources of value.

Among companies that incorporate these value drivers in their business models, which ones are likely to be the most long-lasting? According to Amit, that is hard to predict. In that respect, the collapse of Beenz.com and other companies that wanted to create online cash offers an instructive example.

On the surface, Beenz.com's business model seemed sound. Launched by Charles Cohen, a former speechwriter for Britain's Liberal Democrats, the company succeeded in attracting widespread support from investors. Its business model was intended to encourage efficiency. As *The Guardian* observes, "Beenz.com was a loyalty programme awarding Internet users points across all member Web sites. The idea had come about because of the amount of plastic in Cohen's wallet. Each card awarded its own loyalty points that individually amounted to nothing. 'It spread very quickly and excited a lot of people. It was a grand idea with a capital G,' he says."[10]

In addition to efficiency, the Beenz.com business model also appeared to have complementarities (because it allowed the loyalty programs to be bundled together), lock-in (because beenz users built reserves of loyalty points that "locked" them into having to use them), and novelty (because the idea of a Web-based currency was undoubtedly innovative). These factors spurred initial growth at Beenz.com. The company's brand was advertised from London to San Francisco, and it had more than 300 employees who worked out of 13 offices around the world.

Problems appeared almost immediately, however. The fundamental problem was, as Webvan discovered in a different context,
that Beenz.com was unable to change human behavior. For something to become acceptable as a Web-based currency, it should first
become a liquid medium of exchange for a wide range of transactions—for example, as a means of payment among individuals.
(Some Internet companies, such as PayPal, which was acquired by
eBay in 2002, have tried to go this route.)

Beenz.com, however, could only be used in transactions with
merchants who had joined the system. "The system simply wasn't
flexible enough. You could only use your beenz at merchants: you
could not pay another person with them. You could not buy them
in a 'foreign exchange' market. There was a limited number of
online merchants you could redeem them with and, despite the tie-
up with MasterCard, they did not go far enough to span the physical and virtual worlds," wrote a user. As a result, "People soon ran
out of things to do with their Beenz. This led to a predictable
cycle: a fast uptake, as technologically adventurous people such as
myself created Beenz accounts (in fact, several accounts, since I
kept forgetting my username and password), followed by stagna-
tion (because we could not use the Beenz for much), followed by
indifference."[11]

That indifference eventually proved fatal to Beenz.com—for all
the seeming attractiveness of its business model. By May 2001,
Cohen as well as Donald Maguire, the company's chief operating
officer, had stepped down. Large numbers of employees were laid
off, and joint ventures in Europe and Asia were either put on hold
or wound up. None of these steps, however, could serve as a lifeline. Towards the end of August, Beenz holders were told that their
currency would become worthless and that the company was being
wound up. In an attempt at gallows humor, the *St. Louis Post-Dispatch*

wrote: "If you have any Beenz, it's too late to spill them. Beenz.com, the creator of an online currency that was accepted by hundreds of online retailers, ended operations Sunday. It means that Beenz aren't worth, well, a hill of beans."[12]

In retrospect, the notion that a single company or a few firms— even ones led by dynamic, entrepreneurial individuals—could create a global Web-based currency seems breathtakingly audacious. By contrast, consider how many years of effort it took several European nations to create the Euro—despite the fact that these attempts were backed by central banks and sovereign governments. Such considerations should have led the founders and backers of companies such as Beenz.com to pause. But the dominant mindset during the Internet bubble was that he who pauses, dies.

After the Carlson Marketing Group took over Beenz.com's assets on October 10, 2001, talk about creating a global Web-based currency quietly disappeared. Carlson executives have said that they will use Beenz.com's technology platform and patents for a more modest purpose: to operate loyalty programs for the company's clients. Jim Ryan, CEO of Carlson Marketing Group, notes: "The merging of the beenz patents with our existing proprietary technology opens a whole new frontier in building brand loyalty for our clients, particularly the packaged goods marketplace."[13]

The Beenz.com experience—and that of its rivals, including Flooz.com, which was backed by actress Whoopi Goldberg— shows that while crafting an attractive business model might have been enough to attract venture capital, it is usually not enough to ensure survival. The main reason is because the economic environment is rapidly changing and evolving, and business models often keep pace with these changes.

In general, says Amit, traditional or legacy firms, which combine their online operations with existing offline businesses, are well positioned to draw liquidity (or transaction volume) and take advantage of complementarities and create lock-in. Consequently, we see an e-business landscape in which a growing number of so-called old economy firms will develop powerful e-commerce business models and end up dominating their industries. In addition, say Amit and Zott, "We are likely to witness the integration business models which will once again transform the e-business landscape." Amit and Zott point out that more research will be needed to analyze how business models contribute to wealth creation. Their framework, however, does offer executives tools to analyze how their own e-commerce efforts measure up against these criteria.

In summary, new information technologies have had three effects on competitive opportunities and strategy—the communication effect, the brokerage effect, and the integration effect. Being clear about the effects at play in a particular strategic and market opportunity is very important. Second, three key elements driving competitive advantage are effective positioning in the new opportunity space, creating and leveraging capabilities, and neutralizing the countermoves of competition. Finally, the business model and its robustness in terms of creating value is tested by carefully assessing the vailidity of the sources of efficiency, the role of complementary capabilities in driving the model, and the key elements that lock in customers. The customers' preferences and behaviors can make or break the effectiveness of a strategy.

3

Customer Behavior and Internet Strategies

In the holiday season of 2001, online retailer Amazon.com did something unusual: It offered a 30 percent discount on all books worth $20 or more. Traditionally, books are rarely discounted this way; when booksellers offer steep discounts, these are usually limited to a narrow range of books, such as those on a best-seller list. While some observers wondered how Amazon.com could offer such deals—which included free shipping, in many cases—and still hope to break into the black, Jeff Bezos, Amazon.com's high-profile CEO, defended the move. "Even though it may seem counter-intuitive that lowering prices helps with profitability, we believe it does," he told Leslie Walker, a columnist at *The Washington Post*. "Lower prices lead to higher volumes, which can lead to higher dollar profits even if the percentage profits are less."[1]

Amazon.com's approach raises a broader question. How will customers respond when a company makes an unusual offer, such as offering steep discounts across a wide range of products? If, say, a travel company's online arm were to offer similar discounts on packages including airfare and hotel rates, would customers respond well? What if an investment broker were to offer its clients discounts on other financial services, such as insurance products?

Understanding how consumers will behave is critically important when companies want to establish a Web-retailing strategy. It is useful to develop a framework that can help companies analyze their relationships with their customers. Consumer behavior should be the principal determinant of corporate e-commerce strategy. While technology will improve, consumer loyalty for example is likely to differ significantly between, say, online booksellers and providers of financial services.[2]

Two factors seem critical in predicting behavior and determining an appropriate e-commerce strategy. First, what is the duration of the relationship between the buyer and seller? That is, does the buyer have a relationship with a favorite seller in which they come to learn about each other, or does the buyer search for a different electronic vendor for each interaction? The former suggests an opportunity for tuning offerings; the latter precludes stable relationships. Second, what is the scope of goods and services linking buyer and seller? Does the consumer purchase a single good or service or a bundle of related goods and services? The former suggests that the consumer searches for the provider of the best individual goods and services while the latter suggests a search for the best provider of a collection of goods and services.

Combining these two factors indicates that different companies in different industries will find themselves in one or more of four competitive landscapes.

Consumers buying products that can be described as opportunistic spot purchases exhibit no loyalty; each purchase might be from a different vendor, and there is no one-stop shopping. They might buy a ticket from British Airways one day and United Airlines the next and book their hotels separately.

Opportunistic store markets occur when consumers exhibit no loyalty or relationship continuity to brands or stores. Unlike the spot market, however, they do use intermediaries to construct bundles of goods. They might shop at Sainsbury one day and Tesco another, and they might use Amazon.com one day and Buy.com another.

Consumers buying in categories that can be described as loyal links exhibit continuity when choosing vendors and service providers but have no desire to have bundles prepared for them. They might never leave home without their American Express cards but see no reason for their card issuer to be their insurance provider or financial planner.

Finally, consumers buying in categories that can be described as loyal chains will have preferred providers. Additionally, they will count on these providers for a range of tightly coupled offerings. They might work with a financial consultant at Merrill Lynch who helps pick stocks, reminds them to draft a will, arranges guardians for their children, helps them find a lawyer, and reviews their insurance. The integrated service is so effective that they seldom consider switching providers or taking the time to provide these things for themselves.

Each of these environments has a different competitive feel and requires a different strategy and use of different assets. This situation is as true in the physical world, where companies understand it pretty well, as it is in the dot-com world, where companies are struggling to develop profitable strategies.

No e-commerce company operates in just one environment. There are, for instance, loyal link customers—and companies might pursue them with loyal link strategies—but in reality, some customers might use a Web site for spot purchases and others might show great loyalty. The challenge for companies is to guide the consumer to the behavior matching the company's strategy, and where this action is not possible, companies should match the strategy to the customer's behavior. The approach given here might help managers discover the forces that determine their best strategy.

Opportunistic Spot

Competition in opportunistic spot markets is based on price because there is little loyalty to influence consumers' decisions. This brutal competition is exacerbated by nearly perfect Web-based information. Thus, for standardized products such the latest Harry Potter book, we observe both Amazon.com and BN.com selling at the cost price. Where possible, companies try to soften competition by creating quality differences and ensuring that consumers are aware of them. This branding must be based on real differences, however, because with nearly perfect information it is difficult to deceive consumers. There is a limited role for intermediaries. They might reduce risk in conducting transactions, but in most instances consumers will buy from a set of trusted, well-known manufacturers and service providers.

The Internet will be used for supply-chain management and logistics to ensure the lowest cost structure and the lowest prices. It will also support access to information about consumers, both current and potential new accounts, to enable the most accurate setting of prices where differential pricing is required. That means that no applicant for insurance can be undercharged based on inaccurate risk assessment, and no applicant for a credit card can be given too good a deal. In a market where no one can be overcharged without losing the account, there is little margin for error and little opportunity to recover from undercharging anyone. The ability to predict the profitability of a new customer, and therefore to determine a price to offer, is called predictive pricing.

It is essential to recognize consumers who are exhibiting opportunistic spot market behavior and to develop an appropriate marketing and pricing strategy. For example, in markets that exhibit this behavior, buying market share is unwise because it can be acquired only temporarily. When prices are raised to cover losses, customers will flee. Similarly, a policy of offering selected items below cost as loss leaders to attract traffic would be unwise, because consumers might easily purchase loss leaders from one site and the rest of their items elsewhere. Only time will tell whether the market for books, CDs, or DVDs will exhibit this behavior, so it is too early to assess the validity of Amazon.com's customer acquisition strategy or the promotional items of other Web retailers.

Opportunistic Store

In the absence of consumer loyalty, competition in opportunistic store markets again is based on price; however, it is the pricing of bundles rather than individual items that attracts consumers. Unlike spot markets, there are opportunities for intermediaries to add value through logistical savings (shipping a box of books) or through assembly or integration (selling a package tour or designing a digital imaging platform where camera, printer, and computer work together).

In this scenario, intermediaries enjoy power over manufacturers because consumers select bundles with little attention to components. Thus, when filling an order for paper towels, a grocer will use the product with the highest margins. This pursuit of margins, in the absence of brand loyalty from customers, shifts economic power to intermediaries.

Manufacturers will attempt to use the Web for branding to create consumer awareness of product differences and to weaken intermediaries' power. While it is dangerous to antagonize the existing channel in the opportunistic store scenario by trying to sell directly, branding offers manufacturers the ability to counter some of the power of intermediaries. As in spot markets, manufacturers will also use the Internet to improve efficiency. Intermediaries will use the Internet to create branding for their Web stores, thereby weakening price competition. They will use customer information, as manufacturers did in spot markets, for predictive pricing.

As in spot markets, no consumer can consistently be overcharged, so it is difficult to recover from undercharging anyone. While loss leaders can work in these markets, because a customer might fill a basket or obtain a bundle of services, there is little loyalty to assure repeat business; thus, as in spot markets, buying market share is risky because there is no assurance that initial losses can be recouped by overcharging for later purchases.

Of course, there might be reasons to buy share in a "scale-intensive" industry where volume is needed to bring down unit costs. Indeed, some aspects of online retailing, such as grocery shopping, might be extremely scale-intensive, which could initially appear to justify buying share. Without customer loyalty, however, the danger is that capital will be spent more on training users to accept online shopping and less on training users to accept your online shop.

Loyal Link

Competition in loyal link markets is based on retaining the best customers through a careful blend of service and pricing. For the customer, relationship value and pricing improve over time. For example, anecdotal evidence suggests that online PC seller Dell has succeeded in creating loyal link behavior in customers, many of whom have bought several generations of computers from Dell.

In fact, no incumbent should ever lose desirable business to an attacker. If a less well-informed competitor were to attempt to persuade a loyal customer to transfer his or her business, the current supplier could decide whether or not to match the new offer. If the current supplier, with its detailed knowledge, were to choose not to match the new offer, odds are that the new supplier is making an offer that is too low. Successful attempts to get customers to switch in loyal link markets probably represent pricing mistakes by the attacker. Relationship pricing and value work to soften pure price competition in loyal link markets.

Buying market share will work under certain conditions because it is possible to learn enough to price effectively. Buying market share is ineffective without loyalty, though, as online brokerage firms are discovering—so it is critical to assess whether the company is operating in an opportunistic spot or in a loyal link market.

Using loss leaders in a link market will be unrewarding; offering online banking below cost to gain credit card business is unlikely to succeed in a link market, where customers will pick the best hotel and the best air service or the best online banking and the best credit offers independently.

Systems will be used for branding and attracting customers and to support relationship pricing and relationship service to keep the best accounts. These markets might appear to have only a limited role for intermediaries. Still, intermediaries enjoy an advantage in controlling customer information and might end up owning customer relationships.

Loyal Chain

Competition in loyal chain markets, as in loyal link markets, is based on attracting and retaining the best customers—and, as in loyal link, relationship value and relationship pricing improve over time. In chain markets, however, which are composed of a tightly coupled set of links, pricing to individual customers and the value they receive are determined by a bundle of goods and services.

Taking the earlier example of the digital-imaging platform, it might not be necessary to replace all components when upgrading. If you are buying a higher-resolution camera and a faster laptop, however, it is helpful to determine whether the new computer and the old printer and are compatible; otherwise, the customer might experience an unpleasant surprise if picking and choosing components in a spot or link fashion. If the previous chain supplier is used to update the components, unpleasant surprises are likely to be avoided because his vendor can be relied upon to provide components that are compatible with those bought before. Evidence suggests that Amazon.com has succeeded in encouraging a degree of loyal chain behavior from its best customers who value the book recommendations made to repeat buyers.

Loyal chain markets represent a power shift from producers to intermediaries. Online intermediaries can reconfigure the virtual store to show loyal purchasers the brands that they wish to see, and customers without a preference can be shown brands that earn the highest margins. Indeed, it is a small step from this relationship-based presentation to demanding rebates from manufacturers to ensure that their offerings will be shown to customers who have no brand preference. While physical stores charge a fee for preferred locations such as displays near checkouts, they cannot reconfigure the store for each customer.

This shift in online power greatly increases the importance of branding for manufacturers, because a powerful brand is the best counter to pressure from retailers. It also suggests that to the extent permitted by legislators, manufacturers should form consortia for

Web retailing. This action would avoid a loss of control to retailers that have a significant information advantage. A broad consortium is needed, however, because online markets reward scope and breadth.

Intermediaries can effectively buy market share through pricing low, enabling them to pursue informed relationship pricing over time. Likewise, they can use loss leaders to increase traffic through their Web site, selling other items to consumers who are interested in a complete bundle.

Systems play many roles in chain markets. Intermediaries will use them for branding, to attract customers, and for informed relationship pricing and service. Likewise, manufacturers will use the Internet for branding, thereby limiting price pressure from online retailers. Efficient markets still place significant price pressure on retailers, however, assuring the role of systems for logistics and other forms of cost control. Likewise, manufacturers and service providers will use the Web for their own cost control.

Three observations are true across all four competitive landscapes:

- Only differences between brands, and consumer awareness of them, can blunt pure price competition in an efficient market.

- Cost control is important; efficient access to information makes it almost impossible to overcharge.

- As online information makes markets more efficient, predictive pricing will be used in spot and store markets and relationship pricing will be used in link and chain markets. Pricing strategies will be limited by adverse publicity that companies receive from charging different prices for the same goods.

Other conclusions follow from the following points:

- The role of buying market share will vary. In opportunistic markets, buyers will leave when you raise prices.

- Similarly, the role of loss leaders will vary. In spot and link markets, consumers will pick off loss leaders and do the rest of their shopping elsewhere. Once customer traffic has been acquired, there is a chance to sell extra items.

Companies do face one formidable hurdle, though, before they can reap these advantages. They must pay close attention to the risks that confront them.

4

Managing Risks in Internet Strategy

During the late 1990s, senior executives of traditional companies often viewed the Internet "revolution" then roaring through the economy as French aristocrats 200 years earlier might have regarded the French revolution: as the harbinger of the guillotine. The reasons for their dread are easy to fathom. Established, venerable investment banks and consulting firms, among other companies, were losing hordes of young, bright employees to Internet startups; newspapers and magazines were filled with references to unfamiliar names like Bezos, Omidyar, or Yang; and 20-something CEOs were rising to the top of "richest" lists and being lionized on TV stations such as CNBC. Even more threatening was the fact that fledglings like Amazon.com, eBay, and Yahoo! were worth more on Wall Street than stalwarts like General Motors. It was little wonder that so many CEOs of traditional companies commanded their organizations to develop an e-commerce strategy. What could be more terrible than being disintermediated by a dot-com upstart?

Today, that threat of being swept away by netizens waving the Internet industry's standard (with the bankruptcy of the eponymous *Industry Standard* magazine) has disappeared. The bursting of the dot-com bubble in early 2000, and the technology slump that has followed have taken care of that. This situation does not mean, however, that the risks associated with formulating an e-commerce (or information-based) strategy have vanished. Strategic risks associated with launching e-commerce ventures still exist, and understanding them is crucial.[1]

E-commerce is primarily about commerce, not about "e." Companies want to use electrons to sell physical goods rather than the other way around. Several risks exist in launching e-commerce ventures, but among them, six are most important:

1. **Structural risks:** What if a company designs an e-commerce strategy that, for reasons related to industry structure, cannot be profitable? The reason might be because some e-business plans are so flawed that they cannot succeed. For example, some online vendors of commodity products such as books or CDs sold products on their Web sites at almost the same price it cost them to acquire these products from their manufacturers. Buying *Harry Potter and the Prisoner of Azkaban* for $9.97 and then selling it for $9.97 hardly offers long-term profitability.

   Another aspect of this risk is that for some companies, customer acquisition involves a cost that needs to be recovered over time. In other words, as Webvan tried, it might lose money on initial sales to a customer in the hope that its deals with that customer will become more profitable in the future. If the Internet enables that customer to switch suppliers as soon as costs rise, however, the company might not be able to recover its costs at all. That structural flaw could destroy the company, as it did Webvan and several other dot-com retailers.

2. **Channel risks**: This risk stems from the fact that companies use distribution channels to supply products and services to consumers. For example, manufacturers such as Unilever supply goods such as detergents to shoppers through grocery stores. Vehicle manufacturers sell cars and trucks through dealerships. With the onset of e-commerce, however, it becomes possible for companies to reach customers directly through their own channel without necessarily having to go through an intermediary. The risk, however, is that should a manufacturer try to deal directly with the end user—and in effect, disintermediate the retailer or wholesaler—the intermediaries could retaliate.

Powerful retailers like Home Depot have been able to threaten immediate and effective punishment of any supplier that tries to e-reach consumers directly. Given this risk, for manufacturers the single best play is to strengthen their brands because this action curtails the retailer's ability to steal market share from the manufacturer. If manufacturers do want to reach customers directly and bypass their existing distribution channels, they should consider doing so in partnership with their direct competitors. The reason is obvious: a retailer might be able to punish one manufacturer for setting up a direct channel to service customers, but it cannot punish them all.

For retailers, the best play might be to make the current channel attractive and to gain from the current strength by capturing as much customer preference information as possible.

3. **Sourcing risks**: Substantial risks can arise if a company enters into a strategic alliance with one or more businesses that can

use the alliance to seize substantial value. Imagine a manufacturer of desktop computers that sourced its critical chips and operating system from a single supplier. Which would we expect to make money, the desktop computer manufacturer (IBM) or Intel and Microsoft? With this analysis and the benefit of hindsight, it is not surprising that Microsoft's profits and market capitalization have outstripped those of IBM. The sourcing risk also increases the possibility that a company might become vulnerable to poachers of its intellectual property.

4. **Strategic uncertainty risks:** Some risks of creating e-business strategies arise simply because the future is unknown. This risk is one of strategic uncertainty. Imagine if the oracle at Delphi informed Lord Sainsbury or Wal-Mart headquarters in Arkansas that after the year 2003, no consumer would ever buy shelf-stable products—detergent, paper products, canned beans, coffee, or tea—in a store again but would only shop for these goods online. Would this potential scenario affect the chains' plans for geographic expansion and the construction of new stores?

Such long-term, life-altering uncertainties are strategic drivers. Managers should identify key strategic drivers for their industries. In addition, they should develop a set of alternative futures and develop strategies to deal with each of them by using a powerful technique called scenario analysis, which was originally developed by Royal Dutch/Shell. The detailed planning that companies do to prepare for each scenario exploits their industry-specific expertise for the deployment of their critical economic resources in order to obtain the desired economic outcomes. For example, will customers on the Internet form lasting relationships with their vendors, or will their transactions be driven by whoever offers the best price?

5. **Organizational risks**: Companies that seek to implement e-business strategies must change their organizations to support those initiatives, and all attempts to change organizations have an element of risk. A bank that wants to implement a net banking strategy, for example, might face resistance from managers or employees who do not want to go that route. A failure to execute because people do not understand the strategy can have devastating effects. Equally significantly, some employees might understand why changes are being attempted, might understand all too well what the implications of those changes would be, and might resist them for reasons associated with their own economic well-being. In other words, a strategy is only as good as its implementation—and an organization's capability to implement its strategy involves considerable organizational risk.

6. **Liquidity risks**: The existence of liquidity enables companies to convert assets or instruments into cash and vice-versa. Liquidity makes markets attractive to buyers and sellers alike. Much of the power of eBay, for example, comes from the fact that the company has millions of registered users who buy and sell products by using the company's platform. Once an electronic market has liquidity, it is difficult to dislodge. If the market lacks liquidity, however, it might stymie the most elegant e-commerce strategy. A company's inability to create liquidity by ensuring a minimal critical mass of transactions could land it in a liquidity trap. This issue is critical for so-called business-to-business exchanges, because falling into a liquidity trap could mean gradual irrelevance and eventual death.

As companies try to develop their Internet strategies, they should pay special attention to these risks. Failure to do so could thwart the best-laid strategic plan. Equally important, executives should pay close attention to protecting their intellectual assets—and ensure that they do not fall prey to the risks of a bad alliance—which are as hazardous in business as in matrimony.

Managing Risks in Alliances

Companies often join hands in alliances in order to strengthen their capabilities. As an article in *Knowledge@Wharton* points out, "Like real-life nuptials, many of these corporate marriages—nearly half of them, according to some studies—tend to end in painful separation. Yet a firm that can keep its alliances off the rocks is obviously in a better position to take on its competition. Can companies actually learn to manage their alliances more effectively? The existing literature on the subject is inconclusive, suggesting at most that experience helps: Companies with a longer track record in business alliances seem to manage them better than firms that are relatively new to the game."[2]

According to a Wharton research paper, experience is necessary but not enough for a company to build a successful alliance capability. The paper, titled "Alliance Capability and Success: A Knowledge-Based Approach,"[3] was based on empirical research of the experiences of 140 United States-based companies and found that companies can learn how to manage alliances better through knowledge management or through proactive efforts to accumulate and leverage alliance know-how associated with prior experience.

Companies that practice some of the knowledge-based alliance capability processes described as follows enjoy "on average, an increase of nearly 50 percent in alliance success compared to companies that do not." Hewlett-Packard, Oracle, and Xerox are particularly high performers in this regard.

Managing knowledge of alliance building, the researchers add, will increase capabilities in a range of other strategic areas.

Companies can build and sustain their alliance capability in four ways:

1. **Knowledge articulation.** The skill to manage alliances normally resides in individual employees who have actually done the job. Because these often very personal skills tend to be lost with the lapse of time or employee turnover, it is important that they be converted into some articulated form—such as spoken or written words coupled with the use of metaphors, analogies, or models—from which others can learn. A repository or database can, for example, be created containing the firm's entire alliance history as well as informal and formal debriefings of alliance managers. Hewlett-Packard regularly debriefs its alliance managers so that their personal knowledge is articulated and others have access to their experience.

2. **Knowledge codification.** A company can codify its alliance know-how in guidelines, checklists, or manuals. For instance, Hewlett-Packard has created a 400-page manual that provides codified tools, templates, and other resources for managers in the process of forming and managing alliances. Examples include partner due diligence checklists, negotiation frameworks, draft alliance contracts, alliance termination checklists, company-specific case studies, and so on. Lotus, an IBM subsidiary, has created what it calls "35 rules of thumb" for similar

purposes. The knowledge codification process is different from articulation in that it distills articulated knowledge and transforms it into a form that can be used productively in future alliance situations. So, it is an attempt to transfer past experience to manage similar situations in the future. A hidden danger does exist, however. Codification in books and manuals can hinder managers in idiosyncratic contexts and even preclude efforts to analyze on-going alliance experience.

3. **Knowledge sharing.** Not all prior alliance experience is easy to articulate and codify. Even if it is, the knowledge arising from alliance management is not necessarily spread throughout an organization merely because it is articulated and codified. A process of knowledge sharing also has to be put in place. This process can take several forms: informal conversations and discussions between managers, formal mechanisms such as alliance committees and task forces, and so on. A practice of rotating experienced alliance managers across different collaborative relationships within the firm is another way of sharing alliance know-how. Companies like Corning have created various formal and informal forums for their managers to engage in personal, one-to-one meetings where alliance managers can swap their experiences and exchange war stories.

4. **Knowledge internalization.** Finally, it comes down to people. Individual managers ultimately need to imbibe relevant alliance management know-how in the form of mental models: they have to absorb organizational knowledge into individual knowledge, both tacit and explicit. So the focus is more on having the recipient absorb the knowledge than on having the originator share his knowledge. Training programs and briefings are traditional mechanisms used by companies for

knowledge internalization. Companies like Bell South, Northern Telecom, and others have created in-house alliance training programs and apprenticeships for their managers. In addition, Parke-Davis has a program that attempts to provide alliance-related training not only to senior and middle managers but also to field sales staff if necessary.

Besides these four ways to manage corporate alliances successfully, the researchers also stress the need to build "co-ordinative capacity." This term means setting up a centralized function within a company to deal with all its alliances. Existence of such a capacity can enable a firm to systematically implement the knowledge management processes described earlier. It also enhances the firm's absorptive capacity with regard to alliance management know-how, because the people involved will be in a vantage position to recognize the value of useful alliance management know-how, assimilate it, and then share it across the rest of the firm.

Hewlett-Packard, Oracle, and several other companies have set up a dedicated group to coordinate alliance-related activity within their companies. Organizations that have set up such capacity over time not only are able to form more alliances but also to achieve greater success and value from them. In short, while the knowledge-based approach to managing alliances might not guarantee that corporate marriages will last forever, they do offer a good insurance policy against early divorce.

Protecting Intellectual Assets Against Poachers

A partner today could become a competitor tomorrow. In 1999, Priceline learned this lesson the hard way.

For several months that year, the Connecticut-based company—which enables customers to name their own prices for airline tickets, hotel rooms, and other products and services—discussed a marketing alliance with Expedia, an online travel service that Microsoft owned then and USA Networks owns now. Expedia was keenly interested in Priceline's "name-your-own-price" business model, and Priceline shared detailed technical information about this model with its potential partner during their negotiations.

Later, Expedia backed away from the deal, however, and launched its own Flight Price Matcher and Hotel Price Matcher services, which were almost exactly like Priceline's offerings. Stung by what it regarded as theft of its intellectual property, Priceline sued Expedia and Microsoft for patent violation. After more than a year of high-profile acrimony, the lawsuit was settled on January 9, 2001. While Expedia continues to offer its customers the price matcher services, it has agreed to pay Priceline a royalty for their continued use, according to news reports.[4]

The fight between Priceline and Microsoft is hardly an isolated case. As more companies enter into strategic alliances to extend their competitive reach, the risk that someone—possibly a potential partner or a vendor—could poach their intellectual property is increasing.[5]

Poaching is "the risk that in any contractual relationship, information that is transferred between parties for purposes specified in the contract will deliberately be used by the receiving party for purposes outside the contract, to its own economic benefit and to the detriment of the party that provided the information," according to the paper. While the risk of poaching is hardly new, it is becoming increasingly important in our service-centered, information-driven, post-industrial society.

Two reasons account for this reality. First, many organizations now use contractors for IT-related business services such as consulting, technology infrastructure management, or providing application services and systems development. This has vastly increased the opportunities for poaching in recent years. Second, as more companies outsource service activities to third-party providers such as call centers, they are forced to share immense amounts of sensitive, private information with these service providers. "In both these cases, these data, processes and procedures might have significant resale value, possibly exceeding the value of the contract," the research paper warns.

More risks follow from the nature of intellectual assets. Unlike physical assets, they can neither be returned nor do they get consumed during use. As such, the poaching of intellectual property is often virtually impossible to detect. That is why the risk of intellectual property being poached has not been examined too thoroughly in the past. These days, however, companies that ignore this risk could imperil their future, if not their survival.

How, then, can companies protect themselves against poaching? The first step is to identify the forms in which it can occur. Poaching could take two forms:

1. **Shirking**: This scenario is the classic form of poaching, and it can be found in cases where a principal employs an agent to perform certain tasks. "In cases where effort is costly to the agent and the outcome of the effort is difficult to measure, the agent will exert less effort than is optimal for the principal, thus increasing his or her own benefit at the expense of the principal," the research paper points out.

2. **Hold-up**: This term is sometimes called "opportunistic renegotiation" and involves changing the terms of an agreement due to changes in bargaining power after a contract is signed. For example, once a project has begun, a vendor might try to

change the deal—knowing that the client is unlikely to change boats in midstream.

Poachers versus Poachees

The researchers cite four cases—in addition to the well-known one involving Priceline.com and Expedia—to show how poaching can occur in both service and manufacturing organizations.

First, they point to an instance involving contract manufacturing in the semiconductor industry. According to the researchers, a common practice in the industry is so-called dual sourcing in which a company licenses its technology to a rival so that it can produce competing products for a royalty. The goal of these arrangements is to allay customers' fears of hold-up by the principal manufacturer and to ensure a suitable supply of compatible products, which promotes greater adoption.

In 1982, Intel licensed the technology for its microprocessor to *Advanced Micro Devices* (AMD) as part of a long-term technology-sharing and dual-sourcing arrangement. Four years later, Intel decided that it no longer wanted AMD to be the second source, starting with a relatively new microprocessor line. AMD, however, knowing that Intel might discontinue the relationship and building upon its knowledge of Intel's previous technologies, reverse engineered Intel's microchip and developed a competing product. Intel and AMD are now hostile adversaries in the semiconductor market. In fact, for the third quarter of 2001, even as demand for personal computers and chip prices fell, AMD declared a net loss of $184 million or 54 cents a share and continued a price war against Intel that has bruised both contenders.[6]

Second, they point to a case dealing with contract servicing in the insurance industry. An insurance company hires a third-party account administrator to process and service its accounts—a process that involves sharing detailed customer data. This sharing gives the account administration firm the capability "to mine company data and identify the most profitable customers, which it could pass along as sales leads to competitors or resell to third-party marketing firms," the paper notes. "At a minimum, this could cause a loss of business. In addition, it could also cause substantial reputational damage to the insurance company if its customers discovered that their private information, entrusted to the insurer, was being made freely available to other firms without their consent."

The third case involves a consulting contract in the financial services industry. A credit-card company hires a systems developer to build a complex database to correlate private product-use data with publicly available customer data. The objective is to identify the predictors of profitable customers so that new products can be developed for such clients. The systems consultant builds the database and then—having acquired expertise in developing data warehousing systems for the credit card industry—it proceeds to underbid competitors for work at other credit card companies. It not only reuses expertise but also the actual code from its previous engagement.

"More damaging to the original client, the consulting firm can now pitch this work to competing credit card companies, and with the expertise acquired during its first implementation, it can enable these firms to successfully implement 'copycat' technologies years before they otherwise would have been able to do," the paper notes. The rapid deployment of the same technology by rivals dramatically shortens the period of competitive advantage that the original client enjoys.

The final case is based on a strategic alliance in the travel industry. A large United States-based travel agency that is eager to compete with global firms such as American Express wants to enter new markets in Canada and the United Kingdom. Lacking expertise and relationships with vendors in these countries, the large firm forms an alliance with a small travel agency that has a strong presence in these markets. The small agency hopes to benefit from the alliance by gaining access to the larger firm's global communications network, its client-support software, and so on. A few years later, once the bigger firm has developed the expertise—and name recognition—it needs, it opens an office in the same building and in direct competition with its erstwhile partner. In this case, the bigger firm has appropriated the expertise and exposure that it gained through cooperation.

The small travel agency does not just stand around watching demand for its services vanishing, though. It contacts one of the large company's major competitors and offers to transfer all the expertise it has gained during its former affiliation, thus undercutting some of the large travel agency's competitive advantage. In other words, it responds to poaching by counter-poaching.

"In each of these cases, we observe the essential ingredients for poaching," say the researchers. These include "information transfer, opportunity for reuse of transferred information and damage to the original contributor of information." These cases also illustrate the factors that made poaching both possible and likely. First, the problems in these cases are exacerbated by weak intellectual property protection—and the difficulty of "returning" information once someone else has acquired it. Had suitable intellectual property protection been in place, there would have been legal remedies to reduce the potential for poaching. Even where legal remedies exist, however, actual poaching is often difficult to observe and detect.

In addition, in all these cases the poachers had well-defined markets. There were competitors with similar capabilities who could attain parity or advantage by using the poached information. Poaching is less of a threat absent these complementary assets.

Controlling Poaching

Controlling poaching of intellectual assets can be extremely difficult. The classic remedy to such conflicts of interest is to draw up contracts that align the interests of the vendor and the client or of potential strategic partners. In the case of poaching, however, this solution does not help much because poaching is difficult to detect. One possibility might be to pay vendors based on profitability or other performance measures, but "this is likely to be a very weak incentive when compared to the much larger gains or damage created by poaching," the paper says.

Companies could take certain steps to help reduce the risk of poaching. For example, they could protect themselves against shirking by requiring that their vendors execute performance-based bonds. This regulation would make some resources available to compensate the client in case the contract is not fulfilled, and it would also introduce a third-party arbitrator to oversee whether the terms have been met. This strategy might help in cases where the arbitrator can observe and verify that poaching has occurred.

Corporate reputation offers another possible safeguard against poaching. Reputation is a form of bonding. A firm builds up a reputation over time for engaging in appropriate conduct. Should a firm engage in opportunism that was detected, it would be revealed in the marketplace and its reputation would suffer.

Neither of these methods is foolproof, though. The effectiveness of bonding as a means to reduce the risk of poaching depends on the victim's ability to detect it. This task is extraordinarily difficult to perform in the case of intellectual property. Similarly, the difficulty in using reputation to reduce poaching is that it needs to be credibly demonstrated before the poacher's reputation can be affected. This, too, is rarely easy to do.

Given these formidable challenges, companies might consider exploring new approaches—involving a creative use of technology —to counter the risk of poaching. For instance, sensitive information could be embedded in software or systems rather than being shared with vendors or potential strategic partners. In addition, "confidential data could be encrypted or kept separate from the information that is necessary to reveal to a vendor to perform a service or build a product," the paper recommends. Developing modular products or processes could help prevent reverse engineering. Finally, when large bodies of information (that have potential resale value) are shared with a vendor, they could be seeded with dummy data that might help expose a poacher.

Poaching offers new and formidable challenges as the global economy becomes more knowledge-intensive. It is a newly significant form of opportunism and it represents "the growth opportunity" in e-business white-collar crime. Poaching requires different analytical models and remedies—many of which still need to be developed. Maybe companies should actually encourage poaching of their own intellectual property—but figure out a way to get paid for it.

That is not as incredible as it sounds. After all the legal wrangling, is that not exactly what Priceline.com and Expedia did?

Two
Experience

5

How an Internet-Based Strategy
Affects Financial Services

I n April 1999, representatives of some of the most prominent securities firms in the United States gathered in Philadelphia, PA for a three-day program, the Wharton-SIA Branch Leadership Institute. Co-developed by the Wharton School and the Securities Industry Association, an industry group that represents some 700 securities firms, the annual program aims at improving the leadership skills of high-potential branch managers. As the program's sessions got underway, it was clear that an acute sense of uncertainty —if not fear—prevailed among the participants. Their biggest concern was simple: How would traditional securities firms withstand the onslaught of online trading—spearheaded by upstart dot-com brokerages—that threatened to overwhelm the industry?

In hindsight, it is easy to understand why the growth of online trading worried the traditional brokerage firms. As Mark Lackritz, president of the SIA, explained to those present at the meeting, online brokerage firms enabled customers to trade stocks at low fees, provided around-the-clock access to markets, and made it easy to research information about stocks and companies online. As Lackritz bluntly said, "The paradigm of the industry is shifting. At one time, the securities industry had two monopolies, on information and on execution. Today, both those monopolies are gone."[1]

Viewed in terms of the framework of how the Internet transforms business processes, fast-growing online brokers such as E*Trade and Ameritrade appeared to be thriving as a result of all three effects of the Internet: They made it easy to search for research and data about stocks (the information effect); they made it easy for buyers and sellers to find each other (the brokerage effect); and they also threatened to disenfranchise traditional brokerages that stood in the way of this seemingly dramatic transformation (the integration effect). Little wonder that online trading seemed likely to bring about revolutionary changes not just to the world of brokerage but also to that of financial services in general.

Today, three years later, the changes that the Internet has brought to the world of brokerage and financial services seem to be more evolutionary than revolutionary. With the fizzling out of the dot-com boom and the bursting of the bubble in technology stocks —both factors that drove the increases in trading by individual investors—the discount brokers have seen sharp declines in trading volumes and commissions. Consider Ameritrade, for example, which has emerged as one of the best-known online traders during the late 1990s and is the third-largest online broker after Charles Schwab and E*Trade. The company reported to the *Securities and Exchange Commission* (SEC) that in the first fiscal quarter of 2002, its commissions and clearing fees had dropped 20 percent to $65.7 million. "The decrease was primarily attributable to a decrease in the number of securities transactions as the average trades per day decreased 23 percent to 86,000 in the first fiscal quarter of 2002 from 111,000 in the first fiscal quarter of 2001," the company said. It added that clients were averaging three trades a day rather than five daily trades.[2]

The slow economy of 2001 and early 2002 has aggravated the problems that online brokers have been facing following the dot-com and tech-stock bust. According to a recent report in *The Financial Times* of London, online brokerages are going through a shakeout. Datek Online, for example, merged five of its offices in New York and moved them across the Hudson River into New Jersey. The company was expected to be sold in March 2002; newspaper reports suggested that the bidders included E*Trade and Ameritrade as well as traditional institutions such as Wells Fargo.[3] The formal announcement of the sale came a month later. Ameritrade in April 2002 announced it would take over Datek for $1.3 billion. Charles Schwab, the leading online brokerage firm, has closed operations in Japan and Australia. In addition, Ameritrade has acquired National Discount Brokers, Deutsche Bank's online brokerage arm, while the Bank of Montreal has taken over CSFBDirect (formerly DLJ Direct).[4]

Despite the setbacks, some online brokerages have survived and they seem to be moving toward offering a broader range of financial services. A good example is E*Trade, which on February 13, 2002 announced the launch of its financial center in San Francisco, CA. The company earlier had opened brick-and-mortar offices in New York, Denver, Boston, and Beverly Hills, CA, showing that even an online firm benefits from having a real-world presence. Customers can go to these E*Trade centers to open or review their accounts or work one-on-one with licensed "relationship specialists" who can help them with their financial needs. This concept forms part of E*Trade's strategy to offer its customers "broader, more comprehensive financial services."[5]

Meanwhile, traditional financial services firms such as Merrill Lynch have made the Internet an important part of their operations. In the following sections, we examine why traditional brokerages—which initially tried to ignore the phenomenon of online trading—later adopted it with all the fervor of recent converts. In addition, we look at the case of CapitalOne Financial, one of the largest credit-card issuers in the United States, which implemented an information-based strategy for its credit card operations even before e-commerce became all the rage during the dot-com boom. The lessons of this strategy are all the more relevant as financial services firms try to leverage Internet-based strategies into their operations.

Online versus Traditional Brokerages: The Challenge of Channel Conflict

During the dot-com boom of the late 1990s, discount brokers took to the Internet in great numbers while traditional brokerages such as Merrill Lynch dragged their feet. The reason is easy to fathom. In the case of traditional brokerages, which had legions of account executives who had relationships with clients, the introduction of an online trading service would have been perceived as a threat, and it could have led to broker defections to their competitors.

Merrill Lynch was reportedly losing customers rapidly as Schwab and several others added significant online capabilities to go with their discount structure. At first, Merrill Lynch tried to compete by telling customers what they would be missing (full service) by going to one of the online brokerages, which missed the point badly and did not work.

Finally, after much internal debate, Merrill Lynch decided that it had to have an online presence. This venture was announced in

June 2000, but as part of the announcement Merrill Lynch indicated that the system would not be operational until December 2000, six months away—and an eternity in Internet time. But a strange thing happened: the announcement reportedly stopped the net customer loss. Merrill Lynch went on to implement a reasonably capable online option for its customers, but the firm found that its use has not been as high as might have been expected.

There is a simple point to this story. Customers do not always know what they want, especially when it comes to technology-supported customer service. If they think that they know what they want and you do not provide it, however, you are at a disadvantage. Additionally, customers do not like to be told that you have not given them all the available choices to interact with you. Even if they do not intend to use the channel (online in this case), they do not like being told, "We do not have it because you do not need it." Customers want choices, just because they know that these choices exist elsewhere. In this case the initial *return on investment* (ROI) on the technology investment comes from a defensive analysis—namely, what is the cost of losing customers by not having the technology support that they expect?

Even as they grapple with such issues, companies must make these decisions in ways that help them manage conflicts within their distribution channels. While direct distribution offers several advantages (such as the ability to establish a connection with the customer directly without having to go through an intermediary), it also can be a source of uncertainty. Before trying to distribute its products or services directly to customers and bypassing its traditional distribution channels, a company should examine which products or services lend themselves to be distributed electronically.

Companies should ask themselves three questions to determine whether a market is newly vulnerable to attack. The companies should ask whether the industry is:

- Easy to enter: How easy will it be to enter the channel and attack existing businesses?

- Attractive to attack: Is the market attractive to attack, with the prospect of initial profitability?

- Difficult to defend: Can the existing players defend themselves, and do the new entrant's current distributors and other channel partners have the capability to punish the entrant for launching an electronic attack?

"A channel can become vulnerable if it is easy to enter as a result of a new regulatory change (such as the establishment of the European Common Market, which increased the vulnerability of financial institutions that were previously protected by national borders); technological change (cellular telephony, for example, increased the pressure on Bell operating companies by offering alternatives to their local, land-line-based service); or even consumer preferences (as consumers become more net-savvy, online shopping may threaten established mall operators and the owners of large physical stores)."[6]

When discount brokers such as Charles Schwab began to use online trading extensively, the traditional brokerage business seemed to become a newly vulnerable market. The booming stock market—the *Dow Jones Industrial Average* (DJIA) was hovering close to a major psychological milestone of crossing 10,000 for the first time—meant that many investors felt confident about taking investment decisions into their own hands. Picking winners is relatively easy when the stock market as a whole is rising, which was the case during the boom. That is why discount brokers—with low commissions and fees, whose payment could be readily transferred to the Internet—were the first to take advantage of online trading, while firms such as Salomon Smith Barney and Merrill Lynch hesitated and balked. By 1999, Charles Schwab was handling some 30 percent of online trades.[7] Later, the company's market share grew to more than half of all discount brokerage trading, with 7.6 million online accounts containing $806 billion by March 2001.[8]

In an attempt to defend their turf against upstarts like Charles Schwab, industry stalwarts such as Merrill Lynch announced their own online trading initiatives. Once these firms entered the fray, however, they commanded at least four advantages. David Komansky, then chairman and CEO of Merrill Lynch, explained these during a visit to Wharton.[9] According to Komansky, the following are the four advantages:

1. **Scale matters**: One of the biggest advantages that the Internet operations of traditional financial services firms had over their pure-play dot-com rivals was that they already had an established business base, which gave them advantages in terms of size and resources. "In the business press over the last few years, it was always reported that the small companies could be more innovative, and that to be creative, you had to be small and flexible," Komansky said. "But I feel that if you want to take these ideas and do something about them, you need scale and resources. Before long, only a handful of global players will be able to bring these new ideas to all markets," he said. "Frankly, we welcome that and want to be a part of it."

2. **The brand is crucial**: Another major advantage was that the Merrill Lynchs of the world had proven brand names, while

relative newcomers such as E*Trade and Datek were still trying to establish their brands—an effort that added tremen-
dously to their marketing costs. "I've heard it said that if you
took away all the products from Coca-Cola and left the managers with the brand name, they could build up the company
again in five years," Komansky said. "But, if you took away the
brand and left them with the products, they would be out of
business in those same five years. New or old economy, brand
still matters."

3. **Relationships are critical**: Sales in most industries are based
   on relationships of trust between buyers and sellers, but in
   few industries do trust and relationships matter as much as in
   financial services. In this area, established companies that had
   spent years cultivating the confidence of their clients had an
   edge in carrying over these relationships to the online world.
   Komansky noted that "In a world filled with information, relationships are critical. Financial services companies that only
   offer online services will find themselves falling off. There
   may be a lot of information for the consumer, but he or she is
   still looking for someone with integrity to interpret it." While
   Komansky admitted that "Merrill Lynch had to start an online
   service to compete with Schwab," he added that "young customers these days who trade online will, in a few years, want
   a trusted firm to manage his or her assets."

4. **Seizing opportunity matters more than age**: "I give a lot of
   credit to Amazon and Dell and Yahoo. Those companies
   found new ways of buying and selling that are quite important," Komansky said. "But neither should we assume that
   with the dot-coms crashing, [only] old companies will thrive.

Old or new, the news, as it has always been, is to not only see what is next, but to have the resources to accomplish it."

Information-Based Strategy in Action: CapitalOne's Experience

The slow economy following the dot-com collapse has not treated many companies kindly. In addition to Enron, which exploded in an unprecedented destruction of value, stalwarts such as Kmart and Tyco fell from grace. In this tough economic environment, however, CapitalOne—which is headquartered in Falls Church, Virginia, continues to claim rapid growth. On January 15, 2002, the company announced that it had had a banner year in 2001, with earnings growing to $642 million—an increase of 30 percent over $470 million in 2000. Richard D. Fairbank, CapitalOne's CEO, said that he expected growth to continue during 2002 and that "despite the uncertainty concerning the strength and timing of an economic recovery, we expect to achieve our 20 percent earnings per share growth target in 2002."[10]

In CapitalOne's case, these growth rate numbers are the rule rather than the exception. During the past decade, the company has not only seen rapid growth but also a default rate that is among the lowest in the industry—approximately 4 percent compared with an industry average of 5 percent to 6 percent.[11] This scenario has given CapitalOne enormous financial clout—its managed consumer loan balances in January 2002 exceeded $45 billion—as well as a massive consumer base. "We've created one of the largest customer franchises with more than 43 million customers," says Nigel Morris, president of CapitalOne.[12]

What makes CapitalOne's experience relevant is not just the fact that it has achieved such rapid growth but the way in which it was achieved. From its inception as a division of Signet Bank, CapitalOne has employed what it describes as an information-based strategy to exploit "fundamental differences between itself and its competitors in organizational structure, corporate culture, and use of information. Fairbank and Morris define information-based strategy as the use of scientific tests to drive mass customization."[13] Morris explained the gist of CapitalOne's information-based strategy in a magazine interview in October 2001. "The credit card business is a ferociously competitive business—more so in the United States than it is anywhere else," he said. "Information lets us target the right target to the right customer at the right time and at the right price. Our ability to harness and synthesize that information is the lifeblood of our business. Our future depends on our ability to continue to be a leader in information management and customer targeting."[14]

In other words, CapitalOne's strategy is based on its belief that it is not in the credit card business but rather in the business of managing information. As such, its strategy is applicable to other industries where customers, in their regular course of transacting business, provide information about themselves to their vendors. Companies that figure out ways of capturing and organizing this information effectively can gain access to a rich resource, which can be used to offer products or services that can vastly improve their profitability.

How did CapitalOne come up with this strategy? It followed Fairbank's and Morris's realization, during the late 1980s, that in the credit card industry (as in many other businesses) the costs of providing services can differ widely among various groups of customers. For example, "some customers use their credit cards largely as charge cards, paying off their balances in full each month; these customers enjoy the free float, but provide only limited revenues and even smaller profits to their issuers."[15] As a result, some customers are more profitable to serve than others. But because many credit card issuers were unaware who their most profitable customers were, they were vulnerable to competitors who could identify these customers.

Fairbank and Morris "acquired these insights [in the late 1980s] by observing the credit card businesses of many of their major banking consulting clients at that time. [They then] solicited numerous banks as consulting clients to radically transform the credit card business by exploiting these insights. Most banks were not interested in what became known as their information-based strategy, however. In fact, it was not until the first 16 banks rejected their solicitations that they found a home at Signet Bank."[16] At that time banks were uninterested in what Fairbank and Morris had to say about customers and their profitability. They also had one-size-fits-all pricing strategies for their credit card customers. The combination of these two factors helped Fairbank and Morris devise an innovative strategy for Signet Bank, whose credit card operations they were hired to lead. They ran Signet's credit card operations from 1988 to 1994, when Signet's CEO, Robert Freeman, decided to spin off the credit card business into an independent company named CapitalOne.

Fairbank and Morris believed that for credit card companies, the most profitable customers were not those who paid down their balances each month, but those who maintained high balances and regularly made the minimum payments, including the interest rate. As Morris said, "Anyone can find customers who want your money! Anyone can find customers who will take it and not pay you back! The trick is to find customers who will take a lot of your money and pay you back slowly."[17]

For customers who maintain high credit card balances, a key factor is the interest rate because it determines, among other factors, how long it will take to repay the loan. In an attempt to attract such customers, Fairbank and Morris pioneered the concept of offering a low, teaser interest rate to those who transferred balances from other credit cards. Low-interest rates would not attract customers who paid off their balances every month, nor would these rates attract those who had no intention of paying off their balances and who were going to default on their loans or declare bankruptcy. The main target group of credit card users who would find this offer attractive would be those who "will take a lot of your money and pay you back slowly." By offering the balance transfer product, Fairbank and Morris were able to attract the most profitable customers from other credit card companies.

Eventually, the balance transfer product was widely imitated by other credit card issuers and no longer remained profitable, but CapitalOne continued to conduct countless experiments to break up their customers into micro segments and conduct countless experiments to offer differentiated credit card options based on their unique profiles. Once a small test was successful, it could be rolled out more widely.

At the heart of CapitalOne's approach was its enormous database-driven marketing strategy, which tracked customers' demographics and spending behaviors and used this information creatively. Customers provide credit card companies "with tremendous amounts of information when they dine out, rent cars, and travel around the world—using their credit cards every step of the way. [Fairbank and Morris] reasoned that using and testing that information would allow the credit card issuer to tailor pricing, fees and balance limits, and other options—depending on a customer's habits—no matter whether he was high risk or pure platinum."[18]

Many credit card issuers use computers for data crunching. However, "many Wall Street analysts buy CapitalOne's claim that the company has gone way past the somewhat static credit-scoring models used by many lenders. [CapitalOne] has developed a more dynamic tool, one that constantly tracks customer spending habits. Using artificially intelligent computers that learn from each new bit of information—every restaurant meal charged to a customer's card, every car rented, every payment missed—CapitalOne alters the cardholder's credit profile as well as the company's response to that profile—more frequently and precisely than its rivals do."[19]

Having developed the ability to monitor customer behavior and adapt its products to changes in that behavior, CapitalOne has tried to apply its information-based strategy to other industries—as Fairbank once told *The Washington Post*, "This is not about credit cards. This is about changing the world." Two industries that CapitalOne has targeted are automobiles and telecommunications. The company believes it can apply its principles to car loans and cellular telephony; as Fairbank sometimes jokes, "cellphones are credit cards with antennae."[20] The logic is that any company whose product involves monthly interactions with customers can employ data-mining techniques to study what the customers are doing, and then it can use that information to either increase its sales or minimize its risks.

At the same time as it moves into other industries in the United States market, CapitalOne has been attempting to replicate its success in the American credit card market overseas. CapitalOne Europe was established in London in 1996 because the credit card industry in Britain, in many ways, is closest to the United States. Although the European operations have had their challenges—because credit information is treated differently in Europe than in the United States—CapitalOne Europe by November 2001 employed 2,400 people and had more than 2 million customers.[21]

Although CapitalOne has been remarkably successful in employing its information-based strategy, in the aftermath of Enron it has been criticized for not providing more detailed information about its operations. Investment analysts interviewed by *Barron's*, for example, said recently that they had "some concerns about CapitalOne. They have continued to show strong performance, but they have also had very high growth rates, which can sometimes mask underlying trends. Additionally, they do not really give a lot of disclosure, so it's really difficult to evaluate them. You are relying on their assurances that they are using models that can predict how consumers are going to behave. Very often these models do not play out the way they are intended."[22]

Even if CapitalOne were to stumble or fall from its pedestal for some reason, its approach to information-based strategy would not lose its value. Among companies in the financial services industry, it has developed an approach to capturing data about its customers and using this information to develop new products that is the envy of its rivals. As such, CapitalOne's methods offer valuable lessons to executives about how to build value in their own companies and industries.

6

Internet Strategy and the New Media

During the years of the dot-com boom, *The Industry Standard* —an award-winning publication—became compulsory reading for businesspeople who were interested in the way the Internet was transforming business. In August 2001, after some three years of operations, it went out of business. *The Industry Standard's* sudden demise came as a shock to most of its readers, not only because the magazine had high editorial standards (one of the *Standard's* writers won the prestigious Gerald Loeb Award for Distinguished Business and Financial Journalism) but also because it had appeared to be successful as a business.

An article pointed out in *Knowledge@Wharton* soon after Standard Media International, which owned *The Industry Standard,* filed for Chapter 11 bankruptcy on August 27, 2001: "Just last year, the *Standard* . . . set an all-time publishing industry record with 7,558 advertising pages. Some of its weekly issues in 2000 had a back-breaking 300 pages. It made profits in its second year, something few magazines accomplish. And even in the first half of 2001, it was 19th among all magazines in advertising pages, beating out such healthy publications as *Barron's, Newsweek*, and *Martha Stewart Living*."[1]

While *The Industry Standard* paid a heavy price in the media shake-out that followed the bursting of the Internet bubble and the ensu-ing recession, it was hardly the only publication to suffer the consequences of that collapse. Another similar magazine, *Business 2.0*, was acquired by AOL TimeWarner and merged with its newly cre-ated *eCompany Now*—and the combined publication now continues as *Business 2.0*. AOL TimeWarner pulled the plug on *On* magazine, which focused on technology. *Red Herring*, another well-regarded magazine that focused heavily on emerging technology, has slashed staffing and is believed to be seeking a buyer.

The damage has hardly been limited to print publications. Online publications have been hit equally hard, if not harder. To cite just one example, TheStreet.com, whose co-founder James Cramer, a successful hedge-fund manager, had once attacked the business models of "dead tree" publications like *Business Week* and *The Wall Street Journal*, laid off 20 percent of its staff (some 100 people) in November 2000 and closed its U.K. operations in an effort to cut costs.[2] This action was followed by more layoffs in April 2001. According to one account, former CEO Kevin English was negoti-ating the sale of TheStreet.com to *The New York Times* and then to E*Trade before he left the company.[3] (English later became the CEO of Covisint, the auto industry online exchange, but he left that job as well in June 2002.)

Howard Kurtz, *The Washington Post's* media critic, summed up the situation in a column earlier this year when he wrote, "Indeed, there is no shortage of financial woe. Rupert Murdoch's News Corp. is folding its digital media unit, axing 200 jobs. *The New York Times* has cut 17 percent of its new-media jobs and Knight Ridder 16 percent; CNN has sliced 130 jobs. TheStreet.com has fired 20 percent of its staff, NBC Internet 20 percent, CNBC.com 25 percent, and Motley Fool 33 percent. Disney took a $790 million write-off in shutting down Go.com."[4]

The meteoric rise and fall of *The Industry Standard* and the problems at other publications raise the broader question of how media companies can create sustainable value—especially on their Web-based publications. It has long been a truism in the publishing industry that most new publications take several years before they break even and then move into the black. The reason is because in the initial years, the fledgling publication struggles for attention as it gains editorial acceptance. It needs to cross that hurdle and gain a mass of loyal readers before it can hope to attract steady support from advertisers. In traditional publishing, advertisers subsidize the cost of producing and distributing the publication to readers. Although readers do pay subscriptions, the bulk of a media company's revenues come from advertising sales.

During the mid-1990s, when the Internet boom began, media companies set up Web-based versions of their publications that flouted these rules of traditional publishing—encouraged in part by the notion that they needed to "get on the Web" (even if it entailed an economic loss) in order to not miss out on the phenomenon of Web-based publishing. In keeping with the expectations of most Internet users, most online publications—including the online versions of print publications, such as *The New York Times*—gave readers free access to editorial content. This strategy had a two-fold logic: First, these online publications wanted to introduce their editorial content to a younger generation of readers whom they could not reach through their print editions. And second, they also hoped that keeping content free would drive more traffic—or "eyeballs"—to their Web sites, and that this increased readership would help them gain advertising for their Web sites.

New online publications, which did not have counterparts in print, adopted a similar strategy. Many of them assumed that because they did not have to deal with two major costs of traditional publishing—printing and mailing—they could afford to give away their editorial content without charging a subscription fee. Many of them also believed that they had an edge over print publications because they could offer advertisers information that was almost impossible to collect in the world of print publishing. Not only could online publications collect precise data about which articles their readers were reading, but they could also tell exactly how much time was being spent on each Web page, and from where these readers were coming.

Armed with these advantages, online publishers argued that it was only a matter of time before they would gain support from advertisers. These advertising revenues, in turn, would enable them to become profitable companies in "Internet time," provided that venture capitalists and Wall Street were willing to support them in the early stages. Estimates of online advertising by new media analysts seemed to support these bullish views. Typical of those times was the following statement: "Online advertising revenue is expected to more than quadruple to $16.5 billion by 2005 from $3.5 billion in 1999, Jupiter Communications Inc. said in a report released on Wednesday. Despite the widespread talk of softening in the online ad market, Jupiter said online ad spending will grow as businesses look for more efficient and accountable ways to approach marketing."[5]

While some of these beliefs had an element of truth, life turned out quite differently. It might be instructive to follow, in brief, the experience of an online publication that once seemed to have strong chances of success.

TheStreet.com: Struggle for Survival

Launched in 1996, TheStreet.com was once regarded as one of the most promising online publishers of financial news and analysis. In addition to cofounder James Cramer's highly visible and in-your-face style, which gave TheStreet.com its personality, the venture won the support of investors such as Martin Peretz, the owner of *The New Republic*. The New York Times Co. invested $15 million to buy a stake, and Rupert Murdoch's News Corp. also became an investor. From the beginning, the Street.com emphasized strong editorial content. It built a talented team of writers and editors, headed by editor-in-chief Dave Kansas, a former reporter from *The Wall Street Journal*.

Unlike most online publications and the Web sites of most print publications, TheStreet.com adopted a rare business model. Like *The Wall Street Journal's* online version and a handful of other Web sites, it began life by charging a subscription fee for its content rather than just depending on advertising. This approach seemed to boomerang as its rivals—notably CBS MarketWatch—kept editorial content free and were able to attract advertisers. As an article in *The San Francisco Chronicle* noted, "Other sites, such as CBS MarketWatch.com, started giving away financial information. Reuters posted its stories free on the Web."[6] Later, TheStreet.com became a free Web site, and the company developed a companion site called RealMoney.com that charged higher subscription fees and was aimed at finance professionals.

None of this seemed to matter, however, when TheStreet.com went public in May 1999. Its IPO raised $109 million—and its stock, priced at $19 a share, soared to $71. By December 2001, however, the stock was trading at around $1. The company also admitted that it had an accumulated deficit of $132.7 million as of September 30, 2001.[7] In 2001, TheStreet.com lost $29 million on revenues of $15 million. Some of its alliances too have run into problems. The partnership with *The New York Times* has ended, and recently TheStreet.com settled a lawsuit with News Corp.

Today, as TheStreet.com struggles to find a sustainable revenue model, it is betting heavily on subscriptions. In 2001, although advertising and e-commerce revenues came down to $5 million from $13 million a year earlier, subscription revenues were slightly higher: $9 million in 2001 compared with $8 million in 2000. For the future, TheStreet.com is betting that this strategy is the way to go: In the third quarter of 2001, for example, it launched three online products—The Chartman's Stock Picks, The Street Notes, and The Street.com's Era of Value—that will be made available only to paid subscribers.[8]

The editorial challenge confronting TheStreet.com, however, remains strong. Kansas, the editor-in-chief, left the company in the summer of 2001 and recently—in a move that has taken him full circle—joined *The Wall Street Journal*'s online edition as deputy managing editor.

Cramer, too, is considerably less upbeat about financial news on the Internet. Speaking at a conference in Wharton in October 2001, he told "the audience not to watch too much CNBC or read too much of the popular financial press, including his own TheStreet.com. Too many people who appear there, he said, are scripted and do not give enough information to form a basis for real analysis. 'It is ironic that the greatest stock bubble coincided with the greatest amount of information available,' said Cramer, referring to the burgeoning of the financial media and access to data on the

Internet. 'I always thought this would be a good thing, but maybe it was not so good.'"[9]

As TheStreet.com's experience shows, the assumption that online media sites could turn eyeballs into ad revenues and then profits suffers from serious flaws. As the United States economy has slowed and gone into a recession, the problem has become even more serious.

Online Advertising: Lessons from a Pro

The problems of new media companies came up in a conversation *Knowledge@Wharton* had with Randall J. Weisenburger, executive vice president and chief financial officer of the Omnicom Group in New York City, arguably the world's largest marketing communications holding company with more than $6 billion in revenues in 2000. Weisenburger, who worked for First Boston's mergers and acquisitions group after graduating from Wharton in 1987, later headed up the merchant banking operations of the New York City-based investment firm, Wasserstein, Perella. He joined Omnicom in 1998.

Weisenburger believes that the revenue problems of media sites are related, in many ways, to the broader issue of retailing on the Internet. He argues that some dot-coms do have a sustainable revenue model, but most do not. "Now that the IPO and venture capital markets for dot-coms have gone away, some companies have a much greater probability of success than others," he says. "Let me give you an example. Take Amazon. It was a good idea. The company spent a lot of money educating the world that they could buy a lot by simply entering a credit card number on a Web site, and they gave users a lot of tools. In the process, Amazon spent a lot of money just breaking the ice for other online retailers to follow. Amazon got a huge valuation—which was probably too high. But attracted by Amazon's valuation, another 10,000 online retailers developed their own Web sites."[10]

"In response, Amazon had to adopt a cost-cutting model—of selling products for less. People may believe that the Internet is a cheap medium, but it's not a cheap medium at all. In fact, it's fairly expensive—but it is a convenient medium. Frankly, from my standpoint, I'd be willing to pay 20 percent more [for a product I buy off the Internet] because I can buy it at midnight when it is convenient for me, rather than from nine to five, when I am working. I also can't get Amazon's selection in the bookstore in the town where I live.

"So for a lot of reasons, online retailing makes sense. Price may be one of them, but it's not necessarily the best one. Cost-cutting models do not take that reality into account. Online retailers may believe that they are trading the real estate cost for the cost of a few servers—and that one is going to be a lot cheaper than the other—but it may not be. Technology costs money. If you throw $1 billion of equity behind a company, until it runs out of equity it can support a cost-cutting model. But when the equity runs out, that company will have to find a model that works and migrate to it —and then it may have a sustainable business."

Weisenburger argues that this reality has major implications for online media companies. "Some dot-coms believed that if they spent enough money, they could develop content that was interesting enough to bring lots of traffic to their Web sites. They also hoped that they could sell that audience to advertisers for more money than it cost to create that content and the delivery mechanism. The delivery cost of the Internet, however, is not free. If it were, we would not have television or newspapers or radio or billboards. We would have a very clean society and just walk around with hand-held computers.

"But total media spending is going to grow like GDP. You can cut it up a hundred ways, a thousand ways or a billion ways. But if you cut it up a billion ways, the value of that is not enough to support content that is interesting for anyone to go. A lot of people talk about targeting and one-to-one marketing. In theory it sounds great. In execution it does not work yet for a variety of reasons. You might be able to do a little bit of very minor targeting. For example, you might be able to do some negative targeting—which involves eliminating the people you do not want as opposed to narrowing in on people that you do want.

"Let's say a Web site has a million unique users a month. That's a very big Web site; not too many have a million unique users a month. Each user may have 50 page views, so you may have 50 million page views a month. That sounds really big. An advertiser may say, 'That sounds great. I do not mind hitting that audience two or three times a month with my ads, but I'm not going to hit them 50 times a month. Now let's start segmenting those users. How many of the users are men? Does that cut the numbers in half? Maybe I only want men older than 24 but younger than 36, with a certain income level, and so on.' Once you start cutting up those million viewers into 10 sets, which is not terribly targeted, you have 100,000 of them. There's still 50 views each on average, but you only want three. That's a really high friction cost. The friction cost would be 15 percent or 20 percent the cost of the advertising, whereas in broadcast television, the friction cost is probably 3 percent to 4 percent. You are getting a much larger audience. That's the trouble with Web advertising. People have not been able to figure out its effectiveness well. So a lot of work needs to be done.

"It's going to take some time to figure out effective economic models. Web sites with advertising-only economic models will disappear when the equity runs out. They will cut costs until a lot of their infrastructure is gone—and though they will fight tooth and nail until the last minute, ultimately those Web sites will go away. That will increase traffic on the Web sites that survive. Those Web sites may go to a model based on a combination of advertising and subscriptions. If they get a large enough audience, that may work for 100 or 200 sites or some specialty sites around affinity groups. If you are an auto racing fan, you may be willing to pay $2 or $5 a month for a Web site with really interesting material on that topic. Just advertising revenues around that topic would not let a company maintain such a site."

Weisenburger notes, however, that this situation does not necessarily mean that only small, niche players among the online media companies will survive. "It could work for larger sites too," he explains. "For *The Wall Street Journal*, MSNBC, or CNN, their Web sites are a byproduct of what they are doing in print or on television. My son watches football on ESPN and then goes to the Web site to look up the statistics on every player. And he does both at once—it's an interesting dynamic. So for Web sites like that to work, they must either be complete byproducts of other media, or they must have a combination of subscriptions and advertising as independent revenue streams for the creator of the content.

"Quality may suffer in such cases. For example, if you watch the Golf channel [on cable], half the time it looks as though someone shot the picture with a home movie camera—and they probably did. If they improved the production quality of the show, though, the audience is so limited that they could not get enough advertising revenue to have it pay off. If they have free equity it may work for a while, but when that dries up, that model may not work.

"This does not mean that the Internet does not work. The Internet is in all our lives: e-mail, supply chains, brochureware, communicating with your employees, collecting financial information, specific transactional information—and all that is quite interesting. It's just not quite what people dreamed it would be."

Online Content: Will Subscribers Pay?

If Weisenburger's argument is valid, online media publishers might need to develop content for which subscribers are willing to pay a subscription fee, which is what companies like TheStreet.com have begun to do. The question, however, is whether this approach will run into resistance from consumers. Jupiter Media Metrix, a Web usage analysis firm that announced a sale of its research and events businesses to INT Media Group in June 2002, said in a report that it had found that 78 percent of publishing executives said they plan to offer some subscription content by 2003. Sixty-nine percent of consumers, however, said they were unwilling to pay for content on the Internet.[11]

A case in point is Encyclopedia Britannica, which went online in 1994 with a subscription service that grew to reach 75 percent of all United States college students. According to a *Knowledge@Wharton* report, in November 1999 the company began offering free content, assuming that this would draw advertising and sponsorship revenue. "'What changed in 2000 was the economics of that model,' says Tom Panelas, a spokesman for Encyclopedia Britannica. 'When advertising rates plummeted, we decided we needed to diversify our sources of revenue.' Worse, the move to free content cannibalized the company's online business with college and university libraries. Part of the site is still free, but on July 18, 2001, Britannica.com said it would begin charging $50 a year for the bulk of its content. Consumers can get a free two-week trial and so far, the conversion of trial subscribers to paying customers has exceeded expectations, Panelas says, although he would not disclose specific numbers.

"Panelas points out that Encyclopedia Britannica's new premium subscription program is part of a larger strategy to diversify its revenue streams. That includes a greater focus on its more traditional products, such as the first new edition of its 32-volume printed encyclopedia since 1998. 'We put so much emphasis on becoming an Internet publisher in 1998 and 1999 that we now realize it's time to get back to basics,' he says.

"But industry analysts said Britannica.com, and other online services switching to a pay-for-content model, will have problems in an information universe that remains awash in free content. 'I think Encyclopedia Britannica is going to have a very hard time moving into a pay-for-content model. The amount of information available online through a search engine dwarfs what you can find in Encyclopedia Britannica,' says Jim Stroud, an analyst at The Carmel Group in Monterrey, California."[12]

Although Britannica.com's experience is fairly common, it has not been universal. According to one recent report, "*The New York Times* Co.'s Internet operations went cash-flow positive in the second quarter and again in the third quarter, reversing a $23 million loss in the same period last year."[13] Its experience offers clues to other media companies that aim at creating sustainable business value with their Web operations.

How *New York Times Digital* Broke Into the Black

Speaking to *Forbes* magazine, *New York Times Digital* Chief Executive Martin Nisenholtz outlined five key issues that helped *The New York Times* Co.'s Internet operations go cash-flow positive and also make an operating profit of $780,000 in the third quarter of 2001. These included the following:

1. **Aggregating content**: Nisenholtz believes that *The New York Times* Web site is not just an extra channel for *The New York Times*'s journalism. Although readers come regularly to the Web site to read the newspaper's world-class reportage—especially in the wake of the September 11, 2001 terrorist attacks that destroyed the World Trade Center—Nisenholtz sees the Web site as an extension of *The New York Times* brand. As such, rather than focus exclusively on creating unique but expensive content, the Web site has been willing to accept high-quality content from sources such as the *Financial Times* and *CNET News.com*. "We view ourselves as digital merchandisers," Nisenholtz told *Forbes*. "We want to be a beacon or repository for as many (high) quality content feeds as we can aggregate in one place."[14]

2. **Targeting paid content**: Nisenholtz believes that editorial content, like advertising, can be targeted. If this activity is done in ways that add more value to those interested in certain narrow topics, it can help media sites generate revenues. For example, *The New York Times Digital* enables crossword fans to access puzzles on its Web site for a monthly fee of $3.95 or an annual fee of $19.95. The Web site also charges users for access to "premium compilations such as *Glory Days: Baseball in New York 1947-1957*. Die-hard fans pay $9.95 for 12 months of unlimited access to more than 100 pages of archival photos, articles and exclusive multimedia," *Forbes* reports.

    Another example is a compilation that *The New York Times Digital* put together, as part of its "Topics of the Times" section, after author V. S. Naipaul won the Nobel Prize. The compilation included nine interviews with Naipaul and reviews of his books since the late 1970s, and readers were offered unlimited access to this material for a year for $4.95. The "Topics of the Times" section offers similar compilations —for example, selections of articles on terrorism by columnist Thomas Friedman—at the same price: $4.95 for a year's access.

3. **Cutting early**: Nisenholtz said that unlike other online media Web sites, *The New York Times Digital* reduced staffing by 30 percent and cut other expenses before the economic recession hit hard. He and his colleagues re-examined everything they had learned in the previous five years and asked what they would do if they were starting from scratch. That approach helped bring costs closer in line with current economic reality and helped managers rethink work practices that had been set in motion during more optimistic times.

4. **Focusing on repeat readers and advertisers**: Much of the dot-com media focuses exclusively on the total number of readers, total page views, user sessions, and so on. While these are important metrics—because advertisers do take them into account while making media decisions—*New York Times Digital* chose to concentrate on building loyalty among existing readers and advertisers. In practice, this task meant shifting costs away from promotion and new product development to developing a stable readership and creating more effective ad formats for existing advertisers.

5. **Continuing small enhancements**: When trying to rein in costs during austere times, media companies often cut too close to the bone by slashing expenses on content development or infrastructure. In doing so, they end up shooting themselves in the foot. But Nisenholtz and his colleagues

avoided that trap. Instead, they introduced small enhancements on the editorial front—such as the special compilations on baseball—as well as in advertising by introducing new formats such as skyscraper ads, which run vertically on one side of the screen. By doing so, *The New York Times Digital* was able to reduce the risk of readers and advertisers defecting to other publications.

While these five steps are not silver bullets that will enable every online media site to become profitable, they are certainly crucial in one respect: Online publications that ignore these steps will certainly find it difficult, if not impossible, to turn a profit. Although several news organizations have online sites, for now *The New York Times Digital* has a decisive lead over many of them. That does count for something in the uncertain world of the Internet.

A Long-Term View

Skeptics might claim that *The New York Times Digital's* ability to turn a profit does not impress them. After all, they might say, the online publication has two key advantages: top-notch editorial content and an impeccable brand. Given those strengths, it is hardly surprising that *The New York Times* Company is capable of transforming them into revenues and profits. How easy would it be, however, for smaller publications to make money on their online versions?

The answer is that it would be difficult, but not impossible. The *San Diego Daily Transcript* (SDDT), a California-based publication, has succeeded in getting readers to pay for online publication and done quite well for itself. Jan Loomis, a marketing consultant for the publications, explains that the SDDT began looking at digital delivery of editorial content back in 1994, at a time when hardly anyone knew what online publishing was all about. The company set up SD Source, an e-publication that was a unique source and not just a digital copy of that day's newspaper. "Soon, the electronic source overtook print," Loomis notes.

After keeping the online operation open and free from 1994 to 1998, the SDDT decided to start charging its readers for editorial content and for news headlines and summaries delivered by e-mail. At the same time, it moved towards developing an integrated product in the fields of advertising as well as circulation. In other words, a company buying a print ad for the SDDT could simultaneously buy another one on the Web site, and paid subscribers to the print magazine got free access to the Web site and its archive. While company executives had expected to face resistance from both advertisers and subscribers, those fears have been proved groundless. "Some people had made dire predictions, but they did not happen," says Loomis.

Some experts argue that society should be more patient and take a long-term view towards online publications, because value often takes time to emerge. "We are judging online journalism by standards that are not fair," says Sreenath Sreenivasan, a professor at the Columbia Journalism School and administrator of the Online Journalism Awards that are presented each year by the school in collaboration with the Online News Association. Sreenivasan's argument is that when radio and television first emerged as mass media, they had time and space to figure out appropriate business models. Web-based publications—linked at birth as they were with the Internet bubble—are paying the price for that linkage. "Online journals are being criticized for not making money, but good journalism takes time to evolve," says Sreenivasan. "New media publications are not being given any wiggle room; they are being held to harsher scrutiny and tougher standards. That is not right. Henry Luce did not have to answer to the NASDAQ."

7

Post Mortem: Lessons from the Online Stamp Market

I n Fall 2000, as the anthrax scare rippled across the United States, some companies noticed that their customers were reluctant to use regular mail for communications; they preferred e-mail. Franklin Resources Inc. is a mutual fund giant in San Mateo, California, where "the number of customers signing up to receive quarterly account statements via e-mail . . . shot up 50 percent since early October. And Saks Inc., the parent of Saks Fifth Avenue and other retail chains, says customers paying their October bills by e-mail surged 155 percent over August levels," as *Business Week* noted.[1]

Some government departments, too—concerned about being targets of bioterrorism attacks—reacted the same way. For example, "An advisory from the United States *Department of Transportation* (DOT) dated Oct. 19 stated, 'Mail delivery was temporarily halted in the DOT headquarters building, including deliveries for the filing of documents in DOT dockets . . . Those persons making filings in

DOT dockets are encouraged to file electronically by using the DOT DMS Web site.' "[2]

Even before the threat of bioterrorism made the postal service—at least temporarily—an object of fear, the popularity of e-mail was growing rapidly. E-mail, without doubt, is the Internet's killer app. It is among the first services that users get hooked to when they log on to the Internet. In recent years, as people have started e-mailing everything from letters to greeting cards to colleagues, family, and friends, the world has become a smaller place. In fact, traffic on Hallmark.com, the Web site of the greeting card company, was so heavy during the holiday season of 2001 that the company had to turn away people who had come to view free e-cards. Just before Christmas, some customers saw the following message: "Our apologies. We are currently experiencing heavy traffic on our site and are unable to allow additional visits at this time."[3]

As this volume of e-mail explodes, the amount of mail being sent through the postal system—or snail mail, as it is called—should decline, right? Well, the answer is yes and no. The relationship between the two is more complicated than many people realize.

Take America Online, for instance. As the provider of Internet services to some 31.3 million subscribers around the world[4], AOL facilitates billions of e-mail exchanges. And yet, the company is also the fastest-growing user of direct mail in the United States. How did AOL get its 31.3 million subscribers? In large part, it did this by pooling together direct mail lists and using trusted, reliable snail mail to ship several million CDs containing its free software to potential customers. And each time AOL upgrades its software, this deluge of direct mail continues, offering a windfall to the postal service. In fact, the signature message "You've got mail," which AOL e-mail users know well, could apply with complete accuracy to AOL's snail mail.

That insight into the complex relationship between e-mail and paper mail comes from Michael J. Critelli, CEO of Pitney Bowes, a Stamford, Connecticut-based provider of mail and document management services. With $4 billion in revenues derived from activities that include providing postage meters to businesses that churn out massive volumes of mail, Pitney Bowes stands at the turbulent intersection of technologies that threaten to transform the world's postal services. As such, Critelli has thought hard about the impact of technology—and especially the Internet—on the business of mail. He discussed some of Pitney Bowes' experiences in this regard at a conference organized on April 6, 2001 by the Wharton School's Reginald H. Jones Center for Management Policy, Strategy and Organization.

During the peak of the dot-com boom, Pitney Bowes looked like an old economy dinosaur that Web-enabled upstarts would easily drive to its knees. The Internet, according to Critelli, threatened Pitney Bowes's business in three ways. First, the company's core postage meter business was under attack from purveyors of Internet postage. After all, why should anyone rent a clunky meter from Pitney Bowes when stamps could be downloaded much more conveniently over the Web? The second threat, more long-term in nature, came from the possibility that e-mail would gradually supplant letter mail. And the third threat stemmed from the growing view that the Internet would finally usher in a paperless society.

So, did these threats become real dangers for Pitney Bowes, or did they prove to be false alarms? Said Critelli, "Like virtually every major player in the technology sector, Pitney Bowes stock is down from its all-time high. But though I clearly have no occasion to celebrate success, we continue to survive despite these apparent threats." Critelli argued that though the Internet had changed Pitney Bowes's business, it has certainly not overwhelmed it. That, however, is hardly true of the company's would-be rivals.

Consider the first threat: Web-based postage. When companies such as Stamps.com and eStamp came along in the mid-1990s, they bragged that they would revolutionize the mail business by allowing users to download postage from the Internet and print stamps on every printer. "Today, eStamp has exited the business and Stamps.com is on life support," said Critelli. "Even our own Internet postage product, ClickStamp Online, has not produced big revenues." Critelli's remarks, made on April 6, turned out to be prescient; before the end of that month EStamp ceased to exist. Santa Monica, California-based Stamps.com announced that it had acquired "a broad set of patents and other intellectual property rights from EStamp, including the EStamp name and EStamps.com Internet domain."[5]

Why was online postage such a difficult market to crack? In seeking the answer, it is instructive to examine how eStamp and Stamps.com got into the online postage business and why both companies ran into trouble.

What Went Wrong at eStamp?

Founded as Post N Mail in April 1994, eStamp was the first dot-com to attempt selling postage online. Sunir Kapoor, the company's founder, who described his vision at a Wharton conference in December 1999, said his goal in starting the company was to work with the United States Postal Service to sell postage over the Internet. Recognizing that for many users buying postage—not using it—was the most inconvenient aspect of dealing with the postal service, Kapoor said EStamp had developed technology to enable users to download postage into a secure, silver dollar-sized device connected to a PC. Customers could download postage off the Internet at their convenience and print it when they wanted to use it.

Getting the company going turned out to be a major challenge, because it involved convincing postal and federal government officials about the value of the service. Venture capitalists, too, initially expressed no interest in eStamp. Their primary concern was that the United States Postal Service, a much-feared bureaucracy, would not cooperate.[6] Kapoor then took the concept to Microsoft, where he had once worked as a director of worldwide business strategy. Microsoft in 1997 agreed to invest in eStamp, after which the venture capitalists who had earlier shown Kapoor the door changed their tune. In addition, eStamp was able to attract investors such as Compaq and Excite@Home, among others.

On the face of it, online stamps seemed an attractive business opportunity. The United States Postal Service in 1995 had created a certification service called the Information-Based Indicia Program, which enabled companies to sell products or services that could be used as digital stamps. Representing the first new postage program since its approval of the postage meter in 1920 with the launch of this program, the United States postal service opened the doors to online entrepreneurs to enter the $60 billion United States postal market. The postage stamps and postage meters segment— which were used for first class, priority, and express mail—represented $38 billion in annual sales, and that was the market that eStamp and other online stamp providers targeted. eStamp's strategy was to focus initially on the so-called SOHO (small office, home office) market, which was not only large—estimates suggested that the United States in 1998 had 44.7 million SOHO— but also had a high penetration of personal computers. In addition, SOHO businesses were heavy users of postal services.[7]

In practice, however, penetrating the SOHO market turned out to be much more difficult—and expensive—than eStamp had anticipated, although the company partnered with companies such as America Online and Yahoo! in order to increase its visibility and sales. To add to its troubles, in June 1999 Pitney Bowes began a patent infringement lawsuit against the company. Pitney Bowes claimed that it held dozens of patents related to computer-based postage metering, and that eStamp had encroached upon its intellectual property. Kapoor, who had stepped down as CEO a few months before Pitney Bowes sued eStamp, was replaced by Robert H. Ewald, who had worked in senior management positions at Silicon Graphics and Cray Research. eStamp went public in August 1999. In classic dot-com style, its stock soared and traded at more than $40 per share.

Despite the efforts that Ewald and his executive team made to keep eStamp going, the company kept losing money. During 2000, the company lost $112.8 million and had just $5.3 million in revenues, and by November that year, the company announced that it was leaving the Internet postage business to focus on supply-chain execution. By then, eStamp seemed to have lost investors' confidence. The day the company announced it was leaving the online stamps business, its stock was down to 28 cents.

Commenting on eStamp's decision, Peter Grant, an analyst with the Gartner Group, said that one of the company's most serious problems was that as the first company "out of the starting gate in the business of online postage, eStamp came up against the inevitable resistance to adoption that any new industry faces." He added that the decision to focus on the SOHO market might also have backfired. "The consumers in the small office and home office markets saw no special reason to give up the convenience and service they have come to expect from the local post office—especially once consumers realized how difficult and time-consuming downloading postage could be," he said.[8]

In other words, eStamp made the same mistake in the online postage business that Webvan made in the online grocery business: It expected that if it offered a different technical solution—such as a secure postage device hooked to the PC—that customers would change their behavior immediately (or at least before eStamp ran out of its investors' equity). That assumption turned out to be wrong (and fatally so).

Though Ewald had spoken bravely about refocusing eStamp's efforts on supply-chain management, the company soon gave up on those attempts. On April 20, 2001, eStamp merged with Learn2.com, an online learning company, and 10 days later it sold its online postage patents and the EStamps.com name to Stamps.com. Though the press release did not mention the price, Stamps.com later disclosed in an SEC filing that it had paid $7.5 million for 31 patents and other intellectual property rights from eStamp.[9]

Stamps.com: A Different Strategy

Although Stamps.com might appear to have won the online stamps battle by taking over eStamp, it, too, had its share of trouble. The company has some 250,000 customers, which puts it in a stronger position than eStamp was, but that positive fact must be weighed against the reality that the company has been bleeding cash profusely. For example, in 2001, Stamps.com had revenues of $19 million, but it lost $209.5 million. In four years of existence, Stamps.com accumulated a deficit of $482.2 million as of September 30, 2001. Unless the company can figure out a way to turn around that situation, its long-term prospects appear to be little better than those of eStamp.

Stamps.com had a different approach to the online postage business than eStamp. Unlike eStamp, which required a piece of hardware to be attached to a PC in order to deliver online postage services, Stamps.com came up with a service based entirely on software. Customers could download software from an Internet Web site onto their personal computers—or load the software from a free CD-ROM. They could then print the digital stamps directly on envelopes or packages and mail them. Simple enough. In terms of ease of use, Stamps.com seemed to have an edge over eStamp.

Although Stamps.com's founders had been investigating the United States Postal Service's Information-Based Indicia Program as early as 1996, Stamps.com was not incorporated until January 1998. The company was first called Stampmaster.com, and it changed its name that December. In February 1998, Stamps.com raised $1.5 million in private equity capital, and by October that year it had recruited its top management team. The CEO was John M. Payne, who had earlier been the CEO of a wireless communications software firm called Armedia. (Armedia filed for Chapter 11 bankruptcy in 1999.)

Having come to the market later than eStamp, Stamps.com followed the typical dot-com path of making deals aggressively. For example, in an attempt to build its online brand visibility, Stamps.com entered into a marketing and distribution alliance with America Online. The company also entered into a deal with Office Depot, an office products retailer, so that visitors to Office Depot's Web site could sign up for Stamps.com's service. It had a similar arrangement with Avery Dennison, a maker of office products and self-adhesive solutions. Eventually, some of these marketing deals turned out to be hugely expensive for Stamps.com, but in the heady, deal-driven attention of those days—when venture capital was flowing freely—few people paid attention to that. By March 1999, Stamps.com had already raised $30 million through private placements of equity, and an Initial Public Offering of stocks was on the way.

When it did come about in the summer of 1999, Stamps.com's IPO was marred by the news that in June Pitney Bowes sued the company—just as it did rival eStamp—for patent infringement. Still, the IPO—when Stamps.com sold more than 5 million shares for $11 a share—was a success. After commissions and underwriting fees, Stamps.com had $57 million in the till. And as news circulated that the United States Postal Service would soon approve its service, Stamps.com's stock kept up a heady climb. Later that year shares reached a high of $88.

At that point, although Stamps.com was losing money—the company was to end that year with $358,000 in revenues and a loss of $56 million—what seemed to count much more with investors was an amorphous quality: momentum. And that, Stamps.com soon showed, it could demonstrate in plenty. On October 22, 1999, Stamps.com said that it had acquired a Bellevue, Washington-based company called iShip.com. iShip.com had developed technology that allowed shippers to compare rates and services among multiple carriers, such as UPS, Fedex, Airborne Express, Yellow Freight, or even the United States Postal Service. One of iShip.com's biggest customers was Mail Boxes, Etc., a franchise network of private post offices, which used the service at some 1,400 locations around the United States. Stamps.com believed that acquiring iShip.com would be a good fit with its digital stamps product because it could add shipping and mailing to its portfolio of services. Stamps.com struck a deal to pay an estimated $305 million in stock for iShip.com.[10]

Barely had the ink dried on the iShip deal when Stamps.com announced another major foray. This time, the company said it had launched a business-to-business subsidiary, EncrypTix, that would enable it to move beyond online postage sales. The idea was to use Stamps.com's secure printing technology—its capability to securely sell postage on the Web—in other types of businesses, such as events, travel, or financial services. For example, just as customers could download postage stamps off a Web site and print them out on their printers, why should not they also be able to download and print movie tickets, airplane tickets, or for that matter, a ticket to a Disney theme park?

The way EncrypTix saw it, a buyer would go to the Disney Web site, pay for a one-day pass at Disneyland in California, and print out the ticket on his or her home computer. The ticket would have a bar code, and when it was presented at the Disneyland entrance, the ticket clerk would verify that it was accurate and wave the buyer through. The same approach could be used with plane boarding passes, checks, gift vouchers, and so on.

Disney was certainly impressed by that logic, because it became an investor in EncrypTix.com. Stamps.com invested $1 million in EncrypTix.com, but several other companies joined as investors, including Sabre Holdings and American Express Travel Related Services. In addition, Vulcan Ventures, launched by Microsoft's Paul Allen, was a major investor, as was Sun American veteran James Rowan. In short order, EncrypTix.com had raised $35 million more in private equity.

By March 2000, a month after Stamps.com's investment in EncrypTix.com, signs began to emerge that the dot-com bubble might have popped. The next six months were incredibly stressful for Stamps.com as the company struggled to translate the eyeballs on its Web site into revenues. When that failed to happen—and costs continued to mount amid minuscule sales—a management upheaval was inevitable.

It came just before the end of the third quarter of 2000. On October 12, Stamps.com announced that John M. Payne had resigned as CEO, as had CFO John LaValle and comptroller Candalerio Andalon. Loren Smith, the company's 62-year-old president, also returned to his primary role as a member of the board of directors. Stamps.com explained later in a statement filed with the Securities and Exchange Commission that in an effort to "more rapidly decrease our operating losses and enhance our ability to achieve profitability," Stamps.com had to implement a new business strategy in October 2000. Apart from the departure of top executives, this strategy also included slashing staff by 40 percent to 315 and combining certain business units.[11] Bruce Coleman, a former CEO of Information Sciences and Walker Interactive Products, was named the interim CEO, and Kenneth McBride became the acting CFO. Marvin Runyon, a former postmaster general of the United States, who had been a member of the board of directors, was elevated to chairman.

As part of the drive toward becoming profitable, Stamps.com took two other steps. First, it jettisoned some of the marketing deals it had struck in previous years, such as the one with America Online. It was when the company announced that it expected to save $27 million in two years by terminating the AOL deal that many investors realized how expensive those deals had been for Stamps.com[12]. Second, the company decided to increase prices. Instead of charging a minimum monthly fee of $1.99 to customers who wanted to download postage off the Web, Stamps.com increased the base fee to $4.99 a month.

Still, when the end of the year rolled around, Stamps.com was awash in red ink. In 2000 the company lost $213 million on revenues of $15.2 million. Realizing that it would need to cut expenses further, Stamps.com laid off another 50 percent of its staff in February 2001—going down to 150 employees. But if Stamps.com executives expected things to get better, they were disappointed. Two more explosions were to hit the company a month later—and both struck body blows.

On March 2, 2001, Stamps.com got word that UPS had bought Mail Boxes, Etc., the most significant user of the iShip.com service and a significant source of revenues for Stamps.com. After taking over the franchisor, UPS proceeded to inform Stamps.com that it would no longer need iShip.com. Secondly, Stamps.com realized that although EncrypTix.com had been greeted enthusiastically as a concept, implementing the deals in practice would take considerable amounts of investment. Unable to contribute more capital to the venture, Stamps.com decided to bite the bullet. EncrypTix.com was shut down.

Without Mail Boxes, Etc., which had deployed a version of iShip.com at 1,400 franchise locations, Stamps.com found it hard to keep its shipping business going. It figured it might be better off selling iShip.com to UPS. The sale was completed on May 18. Although press releases did not mention the amount, Stamps.com informed the SEC that UPS paid $2.8 million for iShip.com—a huge hit, considering that Stamps.com had acquired iShip.com for more than $300 million in stock. The company took a charge of $9.4 million after that sale.[13]

The second half of 2001 saw unstable conditions continue at Stamps.com. In August more layoffs occurred; the headcount came down to 70. Even more significantly, chairman Marvin Runyon and CEO Bruce Coleman left—and McBride, the CFO, stepped into the CEO's role.

Although the company continues to focus on the fact that it has 250,000 customers, some observers believe that some customers might be starting to resist the price increases that Stamps.com introduced last year. According to one report, customers who spend less than $50 a month on postage are annoyed with the change. One of them told CNET News.com, "As little as I use the service, the price increase means it's not worth using any more. I like the service. It's convenient, but not at $5 a month."[14] The company says it knows some customers are unhappy, but argues that in the current economic environment, Stamps.com has little choice but to focus on increasing its profits. It remains to be seen whether this strategy will result in profits, or if Stamps.com, like EncrypTix, will run out of time before that happens.

A Market for Online Stamps?

Given the experience of both eStamp and Stamps.com, does the online postage business have a future? It might, but not in the way that people first expected.

Critelli of Pitney Bowes argues that despite its appeal as an idea, the market for online stamps failed to take off for two reasons. First, its advocates failed to realize how long it takes for change to occur in the heavily regulated postage business. The United States Postal Service, like postal authorities around the world, regulates the mail industry closely to ensure the prevention of counterfeit postage. Operating in this highly regulated environment adds considerably to costs. "Great technology, even if it is affordable and promises real value to consumers, will not succeed if government regulation significantly lowers value or increases its cost," says Critelli. "The United States Postal Service will ultimately find a way to balance its need for revenue security with the need for mailers to have a user-friendly Internet postage product, but that effort will take time and further innovation and may involve deep process changes."

The second reason, notes Critelli, is that for any business to succeed, the cost of acquiring customers and providing them with services must be lower than the revenues generated from transactions
with those customers. In the case of Internet postage, "the cost of
acquiring a single customer was very high—it involved tremendous
advertising expenditures—and revenues were very low." Critelli
claims that some companies paid as much as $500–600 to acquire a
single customer, while the net revenues they got from those customers were in the $3.50 range—clearly not a sustainable business
model. "The broader lesson here is that even well-accepted technologies will fail if the cost of getting them to the customers and
supporting them is too high," Critelli says.

Critelli points out that the threat that e-mail will kill snail mail
has also proved less daunting than Pitney Bowes had feared. "Total
mail volume is still increasing, although some segments of the mail
stream are being affected by e-mail substitution," he says.

According to Critelli, the mail market is divided into segments,
and e-mail has a different effect on each segment. The household-
originated letter mail market constitutes some 10 percent of the
mail stream in the United States. This market has been heavily
affected by the growth of e-mail, but its decline has had almost no
effect on Pitney Bowes, which concentrates on the business market.

Business mail is of two types: It includes transaction mail (bills)
and marketing mail (catalogs, brochures, and so on). Transaction
mail, which makes up 40 percent of the United States mail stream,
has not declined as a result of e-mail. The reasons include the
increase in the number of households in the United States as well
as an increase in transaction activity among consumers. While payment of bills online is growing, this impact has been offset by the
increased volume of transaction mail. "The deregulation of energy
utilities, telecommunications, and Internet and television service

providers are driving a greater number of messages targeted at each customer," Critelli says.

In addition, while electronic bill payment is growing, its growth has been relatively slow. A major reason for this, notes Critelli, is that when companies send out bills to their customers, they usually include a marketing pitch in the same envelope. "Billers look at billing statements as a part of their customer relationship management," he said. Critelli points out that companies are unlikely to let intermediaries consolidate the bill payment business unless they can figure out a way not to lose control over their communication with customers.

Marketing-oriented business mail, which accounts for another 40 percent of the United States mail stream, continues to grow despite the proliferation of e-mail, says Critelli. "The Internet and Internet-based customer relationships are actually stimulating growth in direct mail and will continue to do so," he explains, as the AOL example clearly shows.

The Internet has also spurred an increase in another type of snail mail: package delivery. Companies such as Amazon are shipping out more packages as e-commerce enables them to serve customers in remote locations. Moreover, some 15 percent to 20 percent of goods sold online are returned, which adds to the demand for package delivery. Households, too, are shipping more packages than before, in part because Web sites like eBay permit more person-to-person transactions. In all these instances, the coming of the Internet has stimulated the demand for traditional postal services rather than supplanted it.

As for the future of paper and the impending paperless society, Critelli maintains that this phenomenon is complex. "When I joined Pitney Bowes 22 years ago, people were discussing the paperless society," he says. "I believe paper has a long future." The ways in which consumers interact with paper might change as a result of technology. For example, standalone fax machines have declined in use—a factor that has affected Pitney Bowes's fax business—and copier sales have slowed down. Still, printer sales volumes have been growing fast, largely because business users often send documents as e-mail attachments that are printed out from desktops and because many people print out their e-mail messages to review or file them.

Summing up the ways in which the Internet has had an impact on Pitney Bowes, Critelli says that the Web has dramatically transformed "how we communicate internally and externally." The company uses the Web to communicate more and more with its customers. It is a myth, however, that an increase in Web-based communications will reduce the need for human contact. "We have not seen declines in call-center services," Critelli says. "On the contrary, as products become more complex, customers want high-tech and high-touch contact."

Charles Schwab, the online brokerage firm, has had the same experience. "When Charles Schwab went online, the company believed that the 1,400 employees in its call centers would eventually go away. Schwab now employs 2,800 people in its call centers to support the volume of customer questions about its new products and services. The broader lesson from all this is that the 'virtualness' of an Internet-based or enhanced business model is anything but virtual."

As Critelli navigates Pitney Bowes through these uncertain times, he often remembers a maxim he heard from Ian Morrison, a consultant and author of books such as *The Second Curve—Managing the Velocity of Change*. "Morrison told me long ago that in any revolutionary technology, the pace of change is overestimated in the short run, and the magnitude of change is underestimated in the long run. That is absolutely true of the Internet."

8

Online Exchanges: Do They Have a Future?

Now that dot-coms are no longer in fashion as get-rich-quick stocks, discussions about *business-to-business* (B2B) e-commerce exchanges are rarely heard these days. In a campus version of gallows humor, business school students who a few years ago were hungry for jobs at Internet startups now describe B2B as "back to banking." (B2B's cousin, business-to-consumer e-commerce, has suffered a similar fate: B2C is now "back to consulting.") Still, this development is healthy. The less hype that surrounds B2B exchanges, the more meaningfully their true value can be debated and assessed.

At the height of venture capital-funded hype, B2B exchanges were being touted as revolutionary vehicles that would transform the way in which companies do business with one another. So-called dot-com visionaries waxed lyrical about a new economy where supply-chains would be perfectly coordinated over the Web and where seamless digital interfaces would connect customers with suppliers, dealers, and shippers in vast networks. For companies that did not "get it," why, those old economy dinosaurs would soon get their comeuppance. Theirs would be a fate worse than decapitation: they would be disintermediated.

The typical argument in favor of B2B exchanges was expressed in the following terms, according to Wharton professor Lorin Hitt: The lure of B2B e-commerce stems from its ability to connect massive markets. "All commerce is $47 trillion worldwide, and 60 percent of that commerce is among businesses. That's the motivating argument," says Hitt. Starting from such numbers, those who launch online marketplaces believe that if they can move just 10 percent of these transactions online by 2005, they should be able to capture enormous value. Such entrepreneurs assume that they will be able to charge a fee of 1 percent to 2 percent per transaction, giving their online marketplaces billions of dollars in revenues. Dismissing this argument, Hitt says, "People sometimes forget that 99 percent of transactions take place on the telephone," he points out. "The phone companies get zero transaction fees for these deals."[1]

The reality of B2B exchanges, of course, has been very different. Scores of online marketplaces have folded or morphed into companies with dramatically different business models. The fate of B2B software providers such as Ariba, Commerce One, and Marimba— which in the late 1990s were regarded as high-flyers—has been dismal. While Ariba sold for $180 a share in the summer of 2000, by April 2002 it had slumped to a little more than $3 a share. Commerce One did no better. Its stock price was in the $140 range in October 2000. In April 2002, it hovered precariously at about $1. According to one news report, "Commerce One struggled in 2001 when the market for large, public electronic marketplaces faltered. The e-marketplace software maker laid off nearly half its staff in a major restructuring effort and posted a $2.58 billion net loss for the year."[2]

Despite these problems, however, a few trends are becoming evident in the B2B arena. Wharton management professor John Paul MacDuffie and economics professor Susan Helper of Case Western Reserve University have studied emerging trends in this field, and they recently presented their findings in a paper titled, "B2B and Modes of Exchange: Evolutionary and Transformative Effects." This paper, which forms part of a book titled *The Global Internet Economy* edited by Wharton professor Bruce Kogut, notes that "B2B will be evolutionary rather than revolutionary, and that it will continue to be used in a way that enhances, not replaces, companies' business strategies." MacDuffie and Helper also note that "There has been a distinct shift away from the specialized public exchanges such as Ventro or VerticalNet, and towards large industry-wide exchanges run by consortia of incumbent firms, such as Covisint in the automotive industry and Transora in the consumer products sectors." In addition, "Firms are also drawn to private exchanges, even though these offer fewer potential benefits than the industry-level exchanges that promote standardization throughout a larger network."[3]

In what follows, we examine two issues surrounding online exchanges. First, we look at the fate of public B2B exchanges by looking at the experience of VerticalNet, a Horsham, Pennsylvania-based company that established several of them. Second, we consider the relative success of industry exchanges through the experience of Covisint, an online marketplace backed by major auto companies.

VerticalNet: A Metamorphosis

Few people who log on to the Internet have heard of Solidwaste.com. Compared with portals like Yahoo! or America Online, which lure tidal waves of users each day, Solidwaste.com barely draws a trickle of traffic. Still, for those in the business of treating solid waste, the site offers a source of information about their industry. It features news headlines about landfill closings, auctions for products like carbon steel pulverizers, and reviews of the latest truck-weighing software. It may lack the appeal of Amazon or eBay, but to professionals in its highly specialized field, Solidwaste.com offers, well, solid value.

That, at least, was what Mark Walsh, former CEO of VerticalNet, the Horsham, Pennsylvania-based company that created Solidwaste.com, hoped when he spoke about the company at Wharton at the end of 1999. Since its inception in 1995, Walsh pointed out that VerticalNet had created more than 50 so-called vertical trade communities like Solidwaste.com. VerticalNet's communities included Adhesives and Sealants Online, Hydrocarbon Online and Paint and Coatings Online, among others. (The division that oversaw these vertical trade communities, renamed Vertmarkets, was sold in June 2002 to Corry Publishing.) Unlike consumer-oriented Web sites like Amazon.com or CDNow.com, which aim at individual buyers of books or CDs, VerticalNet's goal was to create virtual business-to-business bazaars, where participants could do everything from exchange basic information to finalize e-commerce deals.[4]

Back in 1999, the B2B market appeared to have vast potential. Forrester Research, a consulting firm in Boston, reckoned that B2B Internet advertising would increase to $2.6 billion in 2002 (from $290 million in 1998) while B2B e-commerce would grow to $327 billion in 2002 (from $17 billion in 1998). B2B online auctions were estimated to reach $52.6 billion by 2002 (from $8.7 billion in 1998). VerticalNet wanted a piece of that action, and Walsh argued that building vertical trade communities represented the way to get it.

Explaining VerticalNet's goals and strategy in a presentation before the Wharton Forum on Electronic Commerce, Walsh noted that VerticalNet's gameplan was simple. "We create, acquire and operate sites on the Internet where businesses interact with each other, access vital information and recreate their industrial communities in the environment of the new media," he said. "As we grow the number of VerticalNet communities, we will grow their value to members, which in turn will increase their value to advertisers and sponsors. This multi-phased growth will result in increasingly higher revenues for VerticalNet."

Walsh had good reason to emphasize revenue growth. Like most Web-based businesses at the time, though VerticalNet had a market capitalization of $5.4 billion, the company was also hemorrhaging cash. In 1998 the company lost $13.5 million on revenues of $3.1 million. Those losses increased—and dramatically so—during during the next two years. While in 1999 VerticalNet lost $53.4 million on revenues of $18.4 million, the following year it lost $202 million on revenues of $112 million.

As a builder of public online marketplaces, VerticalNet was trying to raise revenues from the sale of virtual storefronts. Walsh argued in his Wharton address that he thought over time commissions on e-commerce deals would become a significant cash generator. At the end of the third quarter of 1999, VerticalNet had sold 2,676 storefronts to 1,683 advertisers. The storefronts, Walsh claimed, generate thousands of sales leads for advertisers. "Leads are e-commerce," he said. "Some 20 per cent of VerticalNet's leads have resulted in sales." A recent internal survey found that the average sale on VerticalNet is worth $25,000. In half the cases where deals occurred on VerticalNet sites, the buyer and seller had never done business before.

Former Merrill Lynch analyst Henry Blodget—who has been the target of an investigation by the New York Attorney General's office—was a backer of VerticalNet's strategy, though he argued that the company did not go far enough. In a report, Blodget wrote that "while VerticalNet's storefronts are useful, the company will be truly successful only if it can offer users ways to buy and sell online, generating transaction fees similar to stock brokers' commissions. At present, many VerticalNet users shop online but complete their deals the old-fashioned way, by phone."[5]

VerticalNet tried to stem its losses by replacing Walsh (who remained chairman) with Joseph Galli as chief executive. Galli, who earlier worked for Amazon.com, tried to reorganize VerticalNet into three divisions: one that managed the online exchanges, another that ran the marketplaces and sold storefronts, and a third that provided software to companies that wanted to set up their own exchanges. But the company never quite overcame its problems. Eventually Galli, too, left VerticalNet. Walsh is no longer active in day-to-day business operations at VerticalNet, though he remains on the company's board.[6]

As VerticalNet continues to lose money—in 2001, the company lost $757 million on revenues of $125 million—it has made major changes in strategy. In February 2002, the company announced that its new CEO would be Kevin McKay, a former CEO of SAP America. This change is expected to help VerticalNet transform itself into a provider of enterprise software and collaborative supply-chain solutions. In December 2001 the company acquired a software firm called Atlas Commerce to help it make this transition. Will this strategy work, as of mid 2002, it is too early to say. One positive sign is that VerticalNet in March announced a multi-million-dollar deal with Ikea, the Scandinavian furniture company, to provide a supply-chain solution to improve Ikea's transactions with its network of suppliers. Still, this is an extremely combative market, and as the experience of Ariba and Commerce One shows, success is difficult to sustain.

Covisint: Driving Change in the B2B Auto Market

While VerticalNet aimed at 59 online markets—a vision it has since abandoned—Covisint from the beginning focused on the automobile industry. Created in February 2000 by Ford, General Motors, and DaimlerChrysler, its goal was to form a "single global B2B supplier exchange." To that end, each "company brought together its individual e-business initiatives to avoid the burdens suppliers would endure if asked to interact with redundant proprietary systems. The goal was integration and collaboration."[7]

In June 2002, Howard R. Kuttner, a former group vice-president in charge of worldwide purchasing at General Motors, became Covisint's Chairman and CEO. He replaced Kevin W. English, former CEO of TheStreet.com, who joined the company in May 2001.

Located in Southfield, Michigan, Covisint—which gets its name from Cooperation, Vision, and Integration—also invited other auto companies to join. Renault-Nissan, Toyota, and Peugeot agreed to participate, as did PSA Peugeot Citroën. Oracle and Commerce One came on board as technology providers. An exchange involving such players clearly has enormous market clout. Mark Hogan, president of General Motors' eGM business unit told a Wharton conference in May 2001: "We've already done $1.5 billion in transactions through Covisint. Our goal is to get to half a trillion dollars." Some estimates reckon Covisint's potential volume of transactions is close to $750 billion.

Simultaneously with driving this massive volume of transactions through its exchange, Covisint has three major goals. First, it hopes to promote collaborative product development by harnessing the Internet's communications prowess. Second, Covisint wants to streamline procurement for the auto companies by setting up market mechanisms such as auctions. More efficient procurement would lower transaction and other costs. Third, Covisint wants to streamline the operations of the auto industry's supply chains. As networks of buyers and suppliers interact in virtual space, the exchange's founders hope that the auto industry's work processes will become more efficient and customer-friendly.

It is an ambitious vision. The question, however, is whether Covisint will be able to realize it. Its ability to do so will depend on how Covisint deals with some key challenges.

One major challenge, according to MacDuffie, is that as far as B2B exchanges go, Covisint is "still not the only game in town." Though independent dot-coms that attempted to set up B2B exchanges have all but disappeared, companies such as Honda, Volkswagen, and BMW have not joined Covisint—at least not yet —and could potentially set up rival exchanges. Large auto components suppliers, too, have tried to set up their own exchanges. If competition emerges in the shape of rival exchanges, that could threaten Covisint's prospects. MacDuffie believes, however, that the issues involved in developing a B2B exchange are so complex that even a competing exchange will take a long time to emerge.[8]

A more critical issue is that in order to survive, a B2B exchange must work—and must be seen to be working—fairly for all its participants. Because Covisint is clearly dominated by Detroit's auto giants, it will have to convince other members that it is not simply an oligopsony (a market dominated by a few buyers) bent upon bleeding suppliers.

According to Wharton professor Ravi Aron, in order to avoid this trap Covisint will have to carefully sort through issues of control and ownership. "Who owns the exchange? Who sets the controlling policies? To what extent do buyers control the exchange? These are critical questions," he says. "If an exchange has large numbers of sellers and a few buyers, it means that buyers can exert disproportionate clout. The trouble is that most laws do not deal effectively with such situations."

Fears that exchanges in which rivals come together might encourage collusion or price fixing have prompted anti-trust regulators to closely examine B2B exchanges—including Covisint. In the fall of 2000, the *Federal Trade Commission* (FTC) gave approval to Covisint's plans. MacDuffie points out that if Covisint were to prevent participants from joining the exchange, this exclusion might spark charges of anti-competitive behavior, but Covisint has always made it clear that others are welcome to join. Similarly, he adds, price fixing is difficult without product standardization—and the latter is tough in an industry that abounds in varied brands and models of vehicles. "If GM is buying a seat for a Chevy, Ford cannot buy the same seat for one of its models," MacDuffie says. "These are different products."

Aron argues that a buyer-dominated B2B exchange does not need to overtly fix prices in order to engineer the results it wants. "It is difficult to argue that you are engaged in price fixing when you intelligently choose a market mechanism. If you choose a reverse auction, declare upfront the quantity of a component that you want to procure and make suppliers compete in a downward price spiral, you can argue that you have not fixed any price. What has taken place is dynamic price discovery, not price fixing. That is why the choice of a market mechanism is so crucial." The result of such a reverse auction, however, would be to squeeze prices down for the buyer at the expense of suppliers who bid against one another to get business.

MacDuffie offers a different perspective. He points out that auction-type procurement capabilities are just a small part of what Covisint offers the auto industry. Precisely because many auto components are hard to standardize, "not much of the procurement process in the auto industry is amenable to the auction process," he explains. In recent years the auto industry has seen the emergence of large suppliers that produce increasingly complex and non-standardized modular components for the big automakers. Such products are not commodities—and as a result, they are not easy to sell in auctions or reverse auctions. "Suppliers initially were opposed to Covisint—and they tried to form their own exchange—but then they realized that their products would not be squeezed," MacDuffie points out.

If a price squeeze does occur as a result of reverse auctions or other market mechanisms, the products that will be most vulnerable to them will be standardized items where profit margins are already slender. MacDuffie believes that this, too, is unlikely because Covisint recognizes the danger of pursuing such a strategy. "Squeezing the weakest links of the supply chain is counter-productive," he says. "It weakens your supplier base."

Aron agrees that it will be mainly commodity-type products that will be affected by auction-based market mechanisms. "In direct engineered products, where the level of customization is high, sellers and buyers will both benefit," he says. "If suppliers can find effective ways of customizing their products, the degree of competition among suppliers will decline and the relative gains to buyers also will decline."

Covisint will have to grapple with these issues and more as it moves towards realizing the exchange's full potential in areas such as collaborative production and design. Former CEO English described 2002 as the "make or break year" for Covisint, and he predicted that the company would be profitable by the end of the year. "Last year was the year we built out, restructured Covisint, started to get some revenue going, and we got our act together in respect to our expense levels. We will be a profitable company as we exit 2002," he said.[9]

These are formidable challenges, but then, creating a B2B exchange that is powerful enough to overhaul a giant, global industry's supply chains is hardly an easy task. Still, those who have no stomach for it can always go back to banking.

CONCLUSION
Sustaining Competitive Advantage Amid Uncertainty

W hen terrorist attacks destroyed the World Trade Center and parts of the Pentagon on September 11, 2001, they also created one of the worst kinds of environments for business— one haunted by a sense of uncertainty. More than a year later, the threat of uncertainty persists. The stock markets continue their gyrations, corporate accounting scandals abound, and headlines continue to highlight the rags-to-riches-to-rags sagas of high-flying CEOs. It is increasingly clear that if there were any true winners of the roaring 1990s, they were companies that went about performing careful, controlled experiments in building value, rather than those that bulldozed their way through merger after merger while hiding the true costs of their adventures behind financial trickery.

At such times, it is more crucial than ever to heed the fundamental lessons that emerge from the preceding pages. While the stories and examples in this book might appear very different on the surface, without being trite, they share a few very common characteristics:

The successful examples make economic sense from the beginning and the unsuccessful ones do not. Especially when considering the use of technology to enable business, economics goes beyond dollars and is defined broadly to mean all the things that individuals (and businesses acting through individuals) trade off when making decisions. Money, time, convenience, service, reputation, and quality are all variables that enter the equation.

Information and functional integration are important keys to success. Good strategy that is poorly implemented is especially visible and vulnerable in an electronic world.

Organizational impact is not an afterthought and is an integral part of the strategy to use technology to achieve an advantage. Years ago, in an age when the Internet as we know it today was not even imagined, we talked about the important relationship of strategy, technology, and organization if one was to achieve any impact from IT. This situation is even more important today, and if these areas are considered separately in the planning process, the impact will be marginal.

Internet Strategy: pieces of the puzzle

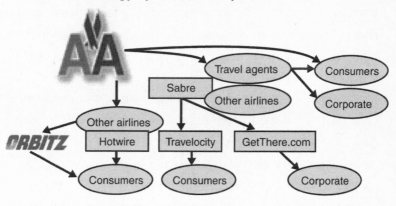

Respect for the value of information and continuing attempts to use it strategically, flexibly, interactively, and with rapid deployment make the difference between winners and also-rans. American Airlines has a long history of using information successfully through its Sabre subsidiary, and that respect for information, along with creativity, has given American Airlines an amazing advantage and presence in all the channels used in online travel today.

Sustaining Competitive Advantage

In addition to these fundamental lessons, executives who want to see their companies not just survive but also thrive in good times and bad must focus on the three key elements or the "competitive advantage triad" that this book highlights. To recap, these factors are:

1. **Positioning in the Industry**: The way a company positions itself in an industry is crucial to its ability to compete against its rivals. Executives must have a thorough understanding of the competitive game in their business, they must recognize the barriers—or absence of barriers—to entry, as well as the key market segments that offer the best long-term opportunities to earn profits. Success often depends upon the ability of companies to change the competitive game in a way that converts its rivals' strengths into weaknesses. For example, IBM's dominance of the mainframe market mattered little to PC manufacturers who challenged its supremacy in the computer industry.

   The fact that companies can integrate the Internet into their operations raises several issues. Among them are questions such as where the boundaries of an industry lie, especially if technology drives them together. Several industries—which in the past were regarded as being separate—are now converging. For example, after the merger of AOL-Time Warner, should the combined company be regarded as an Internet Service Provider (as the independent AOL was) or as a content provider (as Time Warner was)? Such convergences of so-called conduit companies with so-called content companies is just one of the issues with which executives must contend as they go about formulating their information-based strategies.

The well-publicized troubles of AOL-TimeWarner show that these strategies are not only difficult to formulate, but also that their execution may be marred by organizational factors such as boardroom battles.

2. **Leveraging Capabilities**: Companies must build capabilities that allow them to gain an edge over their rivals. Often, it is not the replication of competitors' capabilities, but the introduction of new capabilities that makes all the difference. The ability to sustain a competitive advantage depends upon how long a company can maintain the difference between these new capabilities and those of its rivals. For example, Capital One, unlike other credit card issuers, was able to use its data mining capabilities to make the company grow rapidly in its industry.

Another critical aspect of creating and leveraging capabilities concerns how companies develop and manage their alliances. While several dot-com firms entered into alliances during the heyday of the Internet bubble, many of these were speculative in nature. Some former dot-com executives now admit, for example, that a major goal of some alliances (especially those struck during a company's pre-IPO stage) was to impress potential investors with a view to securing a higher valuation for stock. Apart from such speculative (and potentially deceptive) arrangements, however, companies can use alliances in order to gain several advantages, such as increasing their knowledge about new markets. A case in point is Tesco's decision to partner with Safeway in entering the U.S. grocery market.

3. **Neutralizing Competition**: Sustaining a competitive advantage also depends upon how effectively a company can neutralize its

Summary Table   Key Concepts

Properties of information technology:

	Examples	
Communication effect	Find information fast	Google
Brokerage effect	Link buyers and sellers	eBay
Integration effect	Transform value chain	Covisint

Sources of Competitive Advantage:

A. Positioning in opportunity space		
Market identification		Defense firms
Market segmentation		Capital One
	Data mining	
	Micro segmentation	
Efficiency effects		Amazon.com
Complementarities		Expedia.com
B. Creating, assembling and leveraging capabilities		
Special assets and sourcing opportunities		Coca-Cola
Learning and experimentation		New York Times
Sourcing risks		Wal-Mart
Channel conflict management		Merrill Lynch/Schwab
Building and using knowledge-sharing routines		Capital One
C. Neutralizing Competition		
Customer lock-in		Hotmail
Identifying/influencing the new competitive game		Tesco
Dealing with strategic uncertainty		Merck-Medco

rivals. This strategy refers to a company's capability to defend its position against attacks by would-be challengers. The failure of many dot-coms to survive is closely related to their inability to effectively defend their positions, even though they might have had conceptually strong business models. For example, this factor has been crucial in the online publishing business, where barriers to entry are low. Several online publications collapsed after the established, brick-and-mortar (or rather, paper-

and-ink) publications set up creative Web sites and leveraged the power of the web to support their print products.

In order to neutralize competition, companies must make an objective review of their competitors' capabilities—and those of their alliance partners—as well as their own. Only when they do that can they hope to alter the nature of the competitive game in their own favor.

Monitoring Customer Behavior and Managing Risks

As companies seek to identify and implement strategies that can lead to competitive advantages, they also must pay attention to their customers' behavior. Specifically, this first involves analyzing whether customers want to buy one-off products from the company or whether they would rather purchase a bundle of products. Second, it involves considering whether buyers are opportunistic or loyal. For example, if users of plastic trust Capital One to provide efficient credit-card services, will they also turn to the company when it offers home mortgages and car loans? If customers log on to Amazon.com's Web site to buy the latest Stephen King thriller, will they also order lawn furniture from the company? The success or failure of such efforts hinges on the company's ability to track—and predict—customer behavior accurately.

Executives eager to track consumer behavior could consider four competitive landscapes. The first two are based on whether customers are opportunistic (oriented toward one-shot deals) or loyal (seekers of a long-term relationship with the company); the other two are based on whether customers operate in spot markets (single products) or link markets (chains or bundles of products). Each of these combinations has different implications for managers who seek to draw up an effective business strategy.

Developing information-based strategy also involves managing the risks inherent in Internet projects. These include:

1. **Structural risks**: Identifying and managing structural risks is crucial because it is easy for a company to fall into the trap of establishing a business model that cannot succeed. As noted above, if the value proposition is unclear in the beginning, it will not emerge over time. Possible pitfalls to watch for include strategies whose success may be stymied because of high switching costs.

2. **Channel risks**: Manufacturers can use the Internet to bypass traditional distribution channels and reach end users directly. This, however, leaves them vulnerable to attack by retailers. The power shifts in favor of online retailers from manufacturers, because they gain in-depth knowledge about consumer preferences and choices. Manufacturers can counter this risk by teaming up with their competitors before trying to reach directly for end users. Retailers are unlikely to retaliate against all manufacturers at once.

3. **Sourcing risks**: If a company enters into an alliance with a supplier that allows the latter to become the major source providing that product or service, it exposes itself to the risk of becoming vulnerable to that supplier. An organization that becomes too dependent upon one or more critical suppliers can face a serious threat to its business prospects. Such an organization is particularly vulnerable to poaching.

4. **Strategic uncertainty risks**: Some risks arise simply because the future is unknown. These can be mitigated by using tech-

niques such as scenario planning, which allow companies to anticipate and plan for alternative scenarios of the future.

5. **Organizational risks**: The success of any strategy depends ultimately upon its execution. Organizational risks refer to the fact that even flawlessly designed strategies can fail because of organizational factors that impede their execution. In other words, the risk of doing a bad job is always real. Employees or colleagues may fail to understand and follow the organization's directions. Or, more seriously, they may understand the directions all too well and refuse to follow them.

6. **Liquidity risks**: Internet-based business initiatives can succeed if they can drive enough transactions to ensure liquidity in the market. If they fall into a liquidity trap, these initiatives can fall apart. Online exchanges are especially vulnerable to this risk.

Some Practical Lessons

In addition to the strategic lessons described previously, companies can learn certain practical lessons from the examples in this book. Three of these, which are closely related to one another, seem to be widely applicable. These are:

1. **What you spend on IT infrastructure is less important than what you do with the money.** The recent bankruptcy of K-Mart once again brings into question the difference between K-Mart and Wal-Mart. A few years ago, the rumor was that K-Mart actually spent more on IT than Wal-Mart. Whether that was true or not, it is clear that Wal-Mart

transformed the discount retail business through management of the supply chain, and K-Mart was late to the party.

2. **Creativity matters—be observant and seek out ideas.** Great
processes for planning, lots of infrastructure, glitzy Web sites,
and lots of interaction make no difference if you do not add
value. Figuring out what adds value for the customer and how
to deliver it is the Holy Grail now that we have all gotten
over the "isn't it cool that I can do it syndrome." This situation
is even more important in a business-to-business context.

3. **Creating and adding to shareholder value is the ultimate
evaluation.** Merck recently decided to spin-off Merck-
Medco. Many questioned the combination of the two companies when it occurred early in the 1990s, but it did add value
and is a good example of all of the principles discussed previously. Merck employed detailed measurements to insure that
the return on their IT and Web investments was real.
However, the markets do not always see things in the same
way that management does, and even if something creates
value, it might have to exist in a different form to achieve
maximum shareholder value.

4. **The communication, brokerage, and integration effects are the
drivers.** If you cannot identify where the value added is in terms
of one of these concepts, it will not magically show up later.

5. **Small experiments matter.** Although the Internet has existed
as a technology for decades, its availability as a business
resource is still in infancy. Organizations are still struggling to
understand—and learn from one another—the specific ways in
which the Internet can add value to their operations. And as is
often the case with most forms of learning, small experiments

designed to show what works (and what does not) can be enormously valuable. The speculative bubble surrounding the Internet sometimes obscured this fact, but now that that bubble has burst, companies can focus on gaining small but real insights—the kind that Tesco learned with its first forays into the online grocery market. Over time, these small insights can build up to an enormously valuable perspective on how the Internet adds value to an organization's basic business.

6. **Do not just listen to your customers, study them in depth.** Lots of organizations pay attention to customers and demand patterns in a routine sort of way. If a company does no more than that, it risks remaining at the same level as the rest of its competitors. If true value lies in developing capabilities that go beyond the crowd, companies should study not just explicit customer feedback, but every interaction that implicitly shows what customers want. Capital One's ability to use information *that it already possessed* about its customers made it possible for the company to forge ahead of its rivals. Many companies fail to tap into information they already have about their customers and incorporate it into their product development strategies. This failure is both expensive and wasteful.

7. **Value may lie in microsegments.** During the dot-com bubble, one of the most overhyped features of the web was that it would allow companies to customize products and services for individual customers. While this may have been a laudable goal, in practice many companies have found that customizing and personalizing products and services beyond the most superficial level can be extraordinarily difficult. It also is unclear whether customers actually want highly personalized

services on the Internet. But while customizing services to individual needs may be too complicated and expensive, the Internet does make it relatively easy—as well as cost-effective —to build and create specialized products or services that appeal to microsegments of customers. The ability to target such specialized services at tiny niches of customers can pay off, as the *New York Times* discovered when it created online products for fans of baseball history or the author V.S. Naipaul. In the world of print, a small press run is uneconomical; on the Internet, it is easy to pull off and can work like a dream.

Building Value for the Long Run

In conclusion, one thing seems clear from all the principles and cases of companies that this book has discussed. Although the integration of information and knowledge as essential elements of business strategy is hardly a new phenomenon, the Internet bubble of the late 1990s brought them into sharper focus than before. Unfortunately, at the same time, the speculative bubble also distorted the way in which companies can and should view the Internet and information-based strategy. The two do not stand apart from routine business processes; their true worth lies in creatively blending them with business processes in a way that can help companies maximize value.

Warren E. Buffett, chairman of Berkshire Hathaway, sometimes says that one of the most enduring principles of investment was expressed by "a very smart man in about 600 B.C." The person in question was Aesop, and the principle was that "a bird in hand is worth two in the bush." In his inimitable manner, Buffett adds that only three more questions need to be asked to add to Aesop's insight: What are the chances that there are birds in the bush? How many are there and when will they emerge? And what about the risk-free interest rate? With answers to these three questions, it is possible to measure the bush's value. In his letter to Berkshire investors in 2001, Buffett wrote: "Aesop's investment axiom, thus expanded and converted into dollars, is immutable. It applies to outlays for farms, oil royalties, bonds, stocks, lottery tickets and manufacturing plants. And neither the advent of the steam engine, the harnessing of electricity, nor the creation of the automobile changed the formula one iota—nor will the Internet." Companies that recognize and act upon this timeless wisdom will be best positioned to build corporate value.

Building corporate value is a complex exercise—and business trends during the past three years have made it even more so. In an attempt to help readers gain a deeper understanding of the issues, below appear selected articles from Knowledge@Wharton that shed more light on specific aspects of value building:

1.

Amazon.com & Lands' End: Taking Care of Customers

Knowledge@Wharton, March 3, 2000

Jeff Bezos clearly remembers the Eureka moment that led to the creation of Amazon.com. It was May 1994, and he was working in his mid-Manhattan office, trying to get data about Internet usage. When Bezos found the numbers he was looking for, he was stunned: "Web usage was growing at 2,300% a year," he said. "Things just don't grow that fast. It was a wake-up call."

The rest, as they say, is history. Bezos quit his job that summer, drove from New York City to Seattle, and founded Amazon.com in July 1995. Initially an online bookseller, Amazon now sells 18 million items including CDs, software, toys, video games, etc., etc. Although it has yet to make a profit, its capitalization on Wall Street exceeds that of General Motors. E-commerce is changing the way the world shops, and Amazon.com exemplifies this change as few companies do. *Time* magazine last year named Bezos its person of the year.

Bezos told the story about Amazon.com's creation at Wharton last week when he and David Dyer, CEO of Lands' End—another e-commerce pioneer—participated in CEO Exchange, a public television program moderated by CNN's Jeff Greenfield. Over three hours, Bezos and Dyer shared their strategies and insights, their hopes and fears, with an auditorium packed with students and faculty members. The CEO Exchange program will air on TV later this spring.

Before Bezos launched Amazon.com, he saw it as an online extension of the mail-order business. He listed 20 products that were sold by mail-order and selected books because they were underserved by that marketing process. Bezos was convinced that the Internet would be a good way to sell books—after all, an online bookstore could offer a truly universal selection—but he also had lots of doubts. He told his family, who provided seed capital for Amazon.com, that there was "a 70% chance that it wouldn't work." At the end of the first month of Amazon.com's existence, however, the company, then based in a 400-sq. ft. garage—had orders from all 50 states in the U.S. and 45 countries. "We knew then that customers wanted this," Bezos said. "The rest was execution."

With 20-20 hindsight, what would he do differently about the launch? "We wanted to launch Amazon.com with 1.1 million book titles," Bezos said. "We were advised to launch with 300,000, but we waited until we had 1.1 million titles." In retrospect, Bezos believes that Amazon.com should have launched earlier, even if that meant having fewer books in its catalog. The larger number of books made it difficult for the company to fulfill orders.

As Amazon.com ventures beyond books into other products—the company brags it offers Earth's largest selection of items—it faces a major challenge from Wal-Mart, which this year is expected to significantly step up its online presence. How will Amazon.com respond? Bezos says that the Internet's potential is vast enough to have room for many winners, and different companies will pursue different models toward success. Amazon.com will win if it continues to create value for its customers. In other words, he argues, Wal-Mart's entry need not lead to Amazon.com's demise, which has often been predicted. "We have been called Amazon.toast, Amazon.bomb and, my personal favorite, Amazon.org, since we are clearly not for profit," says Bezos with his characteristic honking guffaw.

So when does Bezos expect Amazon.com to be profitable? Bezos responds that Amazon.com is famously unprofitable principally because it has been investing heavily in the future. "CNN invested for a long time before it turned profitable," he says. "What is different about us is our scale. But there's new new math here." The key, Bezos says, is to focus on creating long-term value for customers.

Like Amazon.com, Lands' End dramatically overhauled its operations to deliver value to customers over the Internet. Although 90% of the company's apparel sales still come from its well-known catalog, CEO David Dyer says that Internet-based sales now account for nearly $100 million in annual revenues. Doing business over the web, he says, is not just a matter of placing "a few product pictures on the web. It is a new way of thinking. We don't think of ourselves as a catalog company. We are a global direct marketing company."

Dyer, whose father and grandfather were retailers, loved the sound of cash registers as a boy, and was determined to find a job in the retail industry. Having worked years ago for Lands' End, he left briefly to join television's Home Shopping Network. Although he returned to Lands' End, Dyer says his experience at the Home Shopping Network was positive. "It is important to make a difference to the place where you work, and also to learn as much as you can," says Dyer.

An avid flyer, Dyer also credits his hobby for having taught him three important lessons. "First, you must always aviate," he says, emphasizing that it is important to fly as much as possible and keep on the move. "Second, you must navigate. Ask where you are and where you want to go. And third, you must communicate." Each lesson has translated well into his business life, Dyer adds.

These lessons served Lands' End well as it developed its online strategy. Dyer believes that companies must fulfill three conditions to succeed in e-commerce. One, it must have a trusted brand. Two, it must have proprietary products with profit potential. Three, it must have efficient distribution channels. "At Lands' End, we had all three," Dyer says, which explains why the company has been able to move 10% of its sales online.

If a recession should strike, will e-commerce companies that are now flying high plunge earthward? Bezos and Dyer have different answers to that question. According to Bezos, Amazon.com has positioned itself as widely as possible primarily to insulate itself against a slowdown in one industry or another. Meanwhile, "the best thing we can do is to invest today," Bezos says. "Taking care of customers today means taking care of customers tomorrow. I always tell our employees, don't be afraid of the competition. Be afraid of the customer."

Dyer says Lands' End, too, has positioned itself to survive a possible recession in the future. "We have 29 million customer names in our files," he says. "This is an asset that is not valued on our balance sheet," but still an important asset. Quoting Warren Buffett, the CEO of Berkshire Hathaway, Dyer says: "In the short term, the market votes. In the long term, it weighs."

2.

Want to Avoid a
Firestone-like Fiasco? Try the M³ Concept

Knowledge@Wharton, September 28, 2000

During the early 1980s, Robert E. Mittelstaedt, Jr., vice dean and director of Wharton's Aresty Institute of Executive Education, was a consultant to the U.S. Nuclear Regulatory Commission. It was shortly after the 1979 Three Mile Island disaster, widely considered the worst nuclear accident in the history of the U.S. "As the Kemeny Commission concluded, the nuclear meltdown was not caused by one mistake, but by a series of mistakes that had taken place over the course of several weeks, ranging from equipment malfunctioning to design-based problems to human error," he says. "If any one of those mistakes had been caught, especially during the early stages of the problem, the accident could have been averted." Mittelstaedt, who is a commercially-rated pilot, has noticed the same pattern in aviation accident reports. "For example, the investigation into the crash of Korean Airlines flight 801 in Guam in 1997 showed that about a dozen separate mistakes led up to that crash.... What you begin to realize, especially in light of such other incidents as the Tylenol tampering scare in 1982 and the Union Carbide chemical leak in Bhopal, India in 1984, is that the same types of compounded errors can occur within corporate systems, organizational structures and processes, with equally dire consequences. The question then becomes how do you, as a manager, prevent this?" The answer, he says, has much to do with "managing multiple mistakes," a process that Mittelstaedt covers in lectures to executives on topics ranging from information technology and strategy to e-commerce and corporate governance. Below, Mittelstaedt explains the M^3 approach.

What do the Firestone Tire crisis, the Watergate scandal, Three Mile Island, and most airline crashes have in common? Quite simply, it would have been almost impossible for each of these disasters to have occurred without a serious chain of unchecked errors leading up to the catastrophe. Whether it is a physical disaster, a political blunder or a serious corporate misstep, the ensuing investigation inevitably reveals that a unique set of errors combined and compounded to make the crisis front page news. The difference between organizations that are portrayed by the media in a negative light, those that are portrayed in a positive light, and those that you never read about in the first place has much to do with the process of "managing multiple mistakes (M^3)."

In each case with crises that have adverse outcomes for those involved, a common pattern exists. First, there is an initial problem, often minor in isolation, that goes uncorrected. Second, there is a subsequent problem that compounds the effect of the initial problem usually in conjunction with an inept attempt at correction. Third, there is disbelief at the accelerating seriousness of the situation. Fourth, an attempt is made to hide the truth about what is going on while efforts at remediation get under way. Fifth, there is a sudden recognition that the situation is out of control, or "in extremis." And finally there is the play-out of the ultimate disaster scenario and recriminations involving significant loss of life, financial resources, or both.

Each day brings new information about the Firestone fiasco, including new attempts at finger pointing and more questions about potential multiple causes intended to diffuse responsibility. Firestone is only beginning to fully understand the severity of this crisis and the long-term threat to their business. In contrast, Johnson & Johnson's successful handling of the Tylenol scare some years ago showed very decisive action and a total commitment to safety, regardless of the cost. Admittedly, removing pain killers from the shelves is different than removing tires and finding replacements. The lack of sufficient inventory to handle the huge demand required Bridgestone Firestone to come up with a phased replacement plan to match manufacturing capacity. One of the company's mistakes was its decision to replace defective tires with other Firestone tires—rather than competitors' tires—because it would cost them less. The correct action would have been for Firestone to immediately recall all the tires and announce that, if Firestone replacements were unavailable, the company would fund replacements offered by their competitors. Unfortunately, Firestone came to this as an afterthought, when it was clear how bad the consequences were going to be. It may well be too late.

Physical disasters such as Three Mile Island and most airline crashes follow similar patterns. Little problems are ignored or misdiagnosed. Failure to act early and decisively results in dire consequences. At TMI, every conceivable human error was made while the system tried to protect itself according to design. The final lapse was when plant operators forgot that water boils if you lower the pressure at a given temperature.

Unfortunately, in the case of aircraft, by the time the problem presents itself to the pilot, there most likely has been a chain of mistakes that should have been broken elsewhere, as this summer's tragic crash of the Concorde outside Paris demonstrated. There is often a slight chance of recovery when disaster strikes during or after take-off, but success is usually dependent on extraordinary skill and luck. Such was the case in the successful dead-stick landing, on an abandoned airfield, of an Air Canada 767 that ran out of fuel in 1983. In that situation, the pilot was able to land with minimal damage to the aircraft based on his skill as a glider pilot and his knowledge of a closed airfield—proficiencies that went well beyond his formal training as a line pilot.

With political mistakes such as Watergate, certain individuals acted in ways that virtually guaranteed that any discovery of the situation would yield results which were increasingly more damaging and required increasingly more elaborate acts of deception.

One can speculate that we will find the same pattern of M^3 failure exposed at some point in the future with Firestone. There are already allegations of manufacturing quality control problems, failure to consistently meet specifications, disagreements over recommended operating parameters and disregard for early warning signs of failures. All that remains is to find out who knew what when and how much was covered up in an attempt to "minimize damage."

What, then, can or should you do as a manager, executive or operator of any piece of a complex organization or machine? The first step is to recognize and acknowledge that the probability of serious consequences from a single mistake is quite low. Most of the world's classic blunders are an unbroken chain of events—an inability to manage multiple mistakes. That is why Toyota auto plants, for example, equip their production lines with red cords that can be pulled by any worker if problems arise on the line. It's easier to correct a mistake early on than face the recall of thousands of defective vehicles or parts further into the manufacturing process.

Second, you need to make M^3 part of your lexicon. The benefit/cost ratio of breaking the mistake chain early in most cases is almost infinite. Third, create an atmosphere that allows mistakes to be discovered and corrected in a positive fashion. Fourth, use case studies and examples to educate others to the danger of not managing multiple mistakes. Fifth, make it the personal responsibility of every individual in the organization to identify mistakes and "stop the production line."

If the steps above sound similar to total quality management, kaizen and other '90s buzzwords, they are. The big difference is that most of the quality movement has historically focused on narrow definitions of processes and errors that are largely physical in nature. Extrapolating the concept to broad organizational and systems concepts is very different than looking for the flaw in the individual widget coming off the production line. What if a series of mistakes in analyzing markets, understanding customers, ignoring feedback and misdirecting investments led you to manufacture the "perfect" widget" whose only flaw was that no one wanted to buy it? This is where traditional definitions of quality and M^3 are very different. Start counting the mistakes that Firestone made and ask yourself how many there are and when they might have been avoided. Then ask yourself, "Is M^3 needed in my organization?"

3.

Real Estate Developers Can Expect
Relocation, not Dislocation, from the Internet

Knowledge@Wharton, January 20, 2000

Some real estate developers see the Internet revolution the same way an aristocrat during the French revolution might have viewed the guillotine. The reasons for their dread are easy to fathom. As more and more CEOs recognize that the Internet is here to stay, they wonder how e-commerce will affect demand for real estate. E-commerce, after all, is about moving business from physical to virtual space and replacing brick-and-mortar storefronts with digital ones. As mainstream Corporate America embraces e-commerce, shouldn't those whose revenues and profits are derived from brick-and-mortar construction fear for their lives?

Not really. Real estate developers and brokers must recognize that the coming of the Internet does not eliminate demand for real estate; it simply changes it, according to academics and industry professionals who met at Wharton recently for the fall members' meeting of the Samuel Zell and Robert Lurie Real Estate Center. Speaker after speaker at the conference—which featured the first Max M. Farash Roundtable on E-Commerce and Real Estate—pointed out that the Internet offers more opportunities than threats to property developers and brokers. As such, real estate professionals would be better off embracing e-commerce rather than ignoring or fearing it.

How does e-commerce change demand for real estate? By way of an example, consider Amazon, the Seattle-based granddaddy of online merchants. The company, which did not exist five years ago and now claims to offer the biggest selection of products on earth, does not occupy a single square foot of space in any mall or shopping center. And yet, as its operations have grown, the company has had to build large stocks of inventory and find warehouses to house them. "Amazon wants to build a fleet of warehouses," says Christopher Peacock, president of Jones Lang LaSalle, a global real estate services firm. In New Jersey alone, Amazon last year was in the market for one million square feet of warehouse space.

That is just one way e-commerce changes demand for real estate. It also changes the skills requirements within real estate companies, which must now increasingly build expertise in technology. "We must help our clients make the right infrastructure decisions," Peacock says. "Our challenge is not just to hire brokers but experts in telecommunications, energy, corporate finance and logistics." Building such skills is crucial as real estate firms seek to redefine their roles for the digital economy. "Success does not begin and end with designing a web page for your company," Peacock adds. "We should use e-commerce to serve our clients."

Jones Lang Lasalle has begun to explore ways of doing that. The company's property management business buys services worth $6 billion from more than 35,000 vendors. In the past, sales orders were typically placed and processed by fax. Recognizing the potential of the Internet to transform the purchasing process, the company decided to move these operations online. Result: Jones Lang Lasalle was able to slash costs by 10%—or $600 million. "That's just one project, so consider the potential," says Peacock. "The future will be even more exciting. I can see a day when the ability to trade in intellectual property relating to real estate will be as valuable as the real estate itself."

Other speakers emphasized that the Internet makes it essential for companies to act fast. One reason is that the web itself has grown—and continues to grow—at an incredible pace. In a presentation on "Forces Shaping the Digital Economy," Gerald Lohse, research director of the Wharton Forum on Electronic Commerce, pointed out that while radio took 38 years and television 13 years to reach 50 million users, the Internet reached that milestone in just five. E-commerce, too, has been exploding. Forrester Research, a consulting firm, estimates that global e-commerce transactions by 2003 will exceed $3.2 trillion. (To put that number in context, Lohse explains, the U.S. economy today is $20 trillion.)

In a panel on e-commerce and retail, Wharton real estate professor Todd Sinai offered another perspective. Discussing whether e-commerce would cannibalize or augment bricks-and-mortar retail, he pointed out that the latter would certainly happen in some markets. "There are places where no one would set up a shopping center, and the Internet can pick up those sales around the edges," he says. In other instances, though, e-commerce sales may not cannibalize traditional retail as much as catalog sales. Time-starved consumers who once browsed through catalogs and ordered products by phone or by mail may now do so over the web. "The Internet is a direct marketing channel," he says.

The Internet also transforms where and how property is built, which means that real estate companies must re-think old assumptions. The maxim that the three most important things in real estate are location, location, and location assumes a new meaning in a global, web-based economy. When business is transacted over the web, producers of intellectual products need no longer be physically close to their customers or even their suppliers. Carrie Byles, an architect with the firm Skidmore, Owings & Merrill, says that if one country's regulations are too onerous, Internet-based companies could easily move overseas or to tax havens. Technology, in many ways, makes location less relevant than it used to be. "For companies like Yahoo, the most important consideration is being close to bandwidth," she says.

Technology also makes it possible for architects to design better environments in which people can work. "We can create offices with casual collision spaces, where new ideas spawn," she says. "Our goal is to create environments that support learning, casual interaction, flexibility and speed in a setting where technology is invisible and the buildings and landscape sustain the human soul."

James Young, president of the Jameson Group, points out that the coming of the Internet is not a short-term change, like the typical 10-year real estate cycle. "This is a major socio-economic shift," he says, comparable in world historic terms to the agricultural revolution and the industrial revolution. The implications for real estate companies, Young says, are clear. "If you sold barns at the end of the agricultural age, you might consider something called a factory."

4.

Opportunities for B2B e-Business in Real Estate

Knowledge@Wharton, November 22, 2000

Last May Chicago-based General Growth Properties, the second largest owner, operator and developer of shopping malls in the U.S., announced an ambitious venture. The company said it would deploy a broadband cable network in partnership with Cisco Systems, the Internet networking giant, to wire together most of the 137 malls it owns or manages in 13 cities around the country. The goal: To give General Growth Properties' retail tenants an "unprecedented competitive advantage by increasing their productivity and operating efficiency." For example, with high-speed broadband connections at the malls, merchants could approve credit card transactions faster, resulting in shorter checkout lines during the holiday shopping season. "Investing in this technology gives us an opportunity to educate our tenants about how they can increase their productivity," says John Bucksbaum, CEO of General Growth Properties.

The alliance with Cisco forms part of General Growth Properties' e-business strategy, which Bucksbaum explained last month at the Fall Members' Meeting of the Wharton School's Samuel Zell and Robert Lurie Real Estate Center. Today, although the stock market's honeymoon with e-commerce has ended, and many dot-coms are closing shop, Bucksbaum still believes that real estate developers must take e-commerce seriously. "Older people may think online shopping is different than shopping in a store, but young people don't differentiate between the two," he says. "To them, it's just shopping. As e-commerce becomes normal, we had better be part of what is normal rather than outsiders looking in."

Bucksbaum's own ephiphany about the potential—and potential threat—of e-commerce came in the summer of 1998, when *Time* magazine ran a cover story exploring how the Internet is changing the way people shop. Online shopping had just begun to take off, and upstarts like Amazon had market valuations matching those of *Fortune* 500 companies. The *Time* article—titled "Kiss Your Mall Goodbye"—predicted a dire future for brick-and-mortar retailers. Seeing the article as a wake-up call, Bucksbaum soon brought together a group of executives to devise an online strategy for General Growth Properties.

The company has spent the past two years investing in technology that integrates the Internet into its operations. "We look upon the mall of today as tomorrow's e-mall," he says. "I see no reason to kiss the mall goodbye. I'd rather kiss the mall hello."

General Growth Properties is using the Internet to change the way it deals with its customers and tenants, as well as to increase its own efficiency. Although this is an expensive exercise, it will pay off in the long run, according to Bucksbaum. In fact, all real estate companies must adopt this approach if they want to survive in the future.

Bucksbaum believes that when real estate companies try to integrate bricks and clicks, "the most important issue to focus on is what you are trying to do. In our case, the most important question was, how do we increase traffic to our malls." General Growth Properties has always tried to "give customers what they want, when they want it and where they want it," notes Bucksbaum, but the arrival of the Internet has changed customers' expectations. Shoppers now want to choose between shopping online or offline. "We went online because we wanted to sell more," he says.

In developing its e-business strategy, General Growth Properties learned crucial lessons from dot-com firms, Bucksbaum explains. "If you buy a book from Amazon, the company uses that opportunity to form a relationship with you," he says. "The next time you go to that website, it will recommend similar books. In our case, although we had 35 million customers visiting our malls each year, we knew very little about them. We knew that the average customer comes to the mall more than 40 times a year, but we knew nothing about him or her. We learned this from e-tailing."

General Growth Properties is betting on its view that investing in high-tech infrastructure will help its retail tenants become more efficient. In addition to speeding up credit card approvals, high-speed cable connections linking more than 100 malls will offer retailers opportunities to do things that would have been difficult in the past.

When a music store in one mall plans a concert, for example, it will be able to offer it by video at other locations. "Using technology to increase the efficiency of retailers helps us strengthen our relations with our tenants," Bucksbaum says. At present, he adds, not one retailer in the U.S. has e-mail that connects all its stores around the country.

Bucksbaum believes that broadband connections at malls will be enhanced by wireless connections over the Internet. For instance, as a customer is walking through the mall, it will be possible to send a message to her cell phone or Palm Pilot about a special on Nike products at the shoe store around the corner. "That is why we have made a big commitment to broadband," he explains.

In addition to using the Internet to redefine its relations with customers and tenants, General Growth Properties is using technology to improve its own efficiency. Once the malls are wired together, Bucksbaum says he plans to eliminate the company's long-distance phone service. "We'll move to voice over Internet," he says. "That will cut our phone bills by $500,000."

Although General Growth Properties is not quite paperless, Bucksbaum is encouraging lawyers to negotiate leases electronically and architects to review plans and blueprints online. The company is also moving toward introducing an Internet-based accounting system. "People have become very innovative," he points out. "These steps will add to our productivity."

Following Bucksbaum's lecture, other sessions at the meeting focused on issues ranging from demographics to entrepreneurial activities.

Demographic Trends and Real Estate

Dougal M. Casey, managing director of Clarion Partners, Adele Hayutin, chief economist of the Fremont Group, and G. Ronald Witten, president of M/PF Research, discussed demographic challenges and opportunities facing the real estate industry. Joseph Gyourko, director of the Zell/Lurie center, moderated the discussion.

The panelists pointed out that ratios of working population to dependent population (defined as those below 15 and above 65) is changing all over the world. In countries like Japan and Germany, the working age population is shrinking, while the dependent population, especially those older than 65, is increasing rapidly. In such countries, absolute population declines are likely. In countries like the U.S., South Korea and Sweden, the workforce is growing, but more slowly than the dependent population. In contrast, young developing countries such as China and Brazil have a fast-growing working population, which outpaces the growth of the dependent population. The conclusion: Think differently about work, the panelists said. "Importing workers will become much more competitive in the future, and worker productivity will become increasingly important."

The panel also discussed the impact of demographic trends on housing demand. They pointed out that age is an important driver of housing choice, and people in their 20s and 50s contribute substantially to demand for rental housing. In the U.S. between 1990 and 1998, the population of single adults grew significantly, which has "favorable implications" for the rental market. The panel also pointed out that during the next five years, all major household growth in the U.S. is expected to be childless. Another major trend, which has been widely discussed for years, is the aging of the baby boomers, which will create massive demand for senior housing.

Forces Shaping B2B E-Business

In his keynote presentation, Lorin Hitt, who teaches in Wharton's Operations and Information Management department, spoke about "The Forces Shaping B2B E Business." Hitt pointed out that fear and opportunities for gain have generated a lot of interest in business-to-business (B2B) e-commerce. The formation of at least 25 major B2B consortia and 700 online marketplaces was announced by last May. Venture capitalists in the U.S., until recently, were aggressively pumping capital into this business. "B2B investments represent 40% of all VC investments, and investment in B2B ventures has grown faster than total investment in venture capital," Hitt points out.

The lure of B2B e-commerce stems from its ability to connect massive markets. "All commerce is $47 trillion worldwide, and 60% of that commerce is among businesses. That's the motivating argument," says Hitt. Starting from such numbers, those who launch online marketplaces believe that if they can move just 10% of these transactions online by 2005, they should be able to capture enormous value. Such entrepreneurs assume they will be able to charge a fee of 1% to 2% per transaction, giving their online marketplaces billions of dollars in revenues. Hitt dismisses this argument. "People sometimes forget that 99% of transactions take place on the telephone," he points out. "The phone companies get zero transaction fees for these deals."

The real value of B2B e-commerce lies in the ability of online marketplaces to offer potential for cost savings. Most of these are achieved by squeezing suppliers through such techniques as reverse auctions (where suppliers bid against one another to meet customer demand). "This doesn't represent an increase in productivity; it is just a redistribution of value," Hitt observes. Online marketplaces also face several challenges. For example, non-standard or hard-to-describe products may be hard to trade through online exchanges. In practice, Hitt warns, although B2B commerce offers the promise of large potential gains, realizing these gains is extremely complex and risky. "B2B e-commerce may also be fundamentally incompatible with some products," says Hitt.

Peter Linneman of Wharton's real estate department moderated a panel about B2B e-commerce in real estate. The participants included Andrew Florance, CEO of CoStar; David A. Hefland, executive vice president of Equity Office Properties Trust; Devin Murphy, managing director of Morgan Stanley Dean Witter; and Scott Rechler, co-CEO of Reckson Associates Realty. Asked whether investors are interested in real estate web ventures, the panelists observed that real estate is well positioned to benefit from the Internet. It is a highly fragmented industry, and as such, B2B markets that aim at overcoming inefficiencies—such as information asymmetries—do have potential. Incumbent real estate companies, which have strong customer relationships in place, are better positioned to exploit this potential than upstart newcomers.

Real estate does face challenges in implementing B2B strategies, the panelists pointed out. For example, while other industries may be able to eliminate intermediaries, in real estate eliminating brokerage firms is hardly easy. "The issue is not eliminating brokers from a real estate transaction, or saving a couple of pennies on a deal where a tenant is paying you $50 a sq. ft., but bringing information efficiencies into the industry," one of the panelists said. The panel also addressed the complicated question of valuing e-business ventures. Their view was that valuation of private companies always involves a negotiation and is fundamentally more an art than a science.

The final panel, moderated by Asuka Nakahara, associate director of the Zell/Lurie center, dealt with entrepreneurship. The panelists said that while technology certainly will play a role in the future of real estate, it will not change the major players in the industry. As such, entrepreneurs should expect technology to bring about an evolution, rather than a revolution, in real estate.

How, then, will value creation in real estate change as a result of technical or demographic changes? Demographics are crucial because they point to emerging opportunities. For example, developers of senior housing are preparing to serve the needs of millions of aging baby boomers. But opportunities abound in several areas, ranging from resorts to affordable nursing homes, the panelists said. Such businesses offer great opportunities in the long run.

Before real estate companies can exploit these opportunities, they face another major challenge: recruiting and retaining their employees. Though the number of those leaving traditional businesses to join dot-com start-ups has waned, real estate still faces a bitter war for talent vis-à-vis other industries. Steps such as offering equity positions in projects or stock options to employees can help nurture an entrepreneurial mindset. "Most real estate projects involve big dollars, and you can't afford to make mistakes," the panelists said. "Offering an ownership stake certainly helps to sharpen your focus. It is a big attraction in recruiting good people."

5.

"E-Commerce Will Transform Supply Chain Management"

Knowledge@Wharton, December 20, 2000

In the early 1980s, IBM faced a critical problem. The company had installed its mainframe computers at customers' facilities all over the world, and it needed to manage its inventory of computer parts in a way that would let engineers fix malfunctioning machines as rapidly as possible. That was a mind-boggling logistical exercise. It involved hundreds of thousands of parts stocked in thousands of locations worldwide.

Even as IBM executives wrestled with the issue, Morris Cohen, a Wharton professor of operations and information management, stepped up to help. As the principal scientist working on the problem, he and a group of colleagues from Wharton helped IBM develop Optimizer, a decision-support system that let the computer giant map out a global parts supply chain. Result: IBM was able to cut inventory investment by $250 million, while reducing annual operating costs by 10% and increasing the level of customer service.

IBM was hardly an isolated case. During the past two decades or more, Cohen has continued to study how companies use supply chains to support after-sales service operations in industries ranging from computers to automobiles. In the process, he says, he has learned fundamental lessons about the way such supply chains should be set up and managed. Among them: It would be a mistake for a company to set up a parts supply chain in the same way that it does its production supply chain. "These logistics problems are very different than planning production," Cohen explains. "They are like high-stakes gambling problems, or like portfolio management problems. You have to solve them by understanding the risk tradeoffs involved."

What exactly does that mean for companies? According to Cohen, one implication is that parts supply chains must be designed in a way that takes into account the criticality of a company's products, and the cost to the consumer if the product fails. Consider, for example, a component in a computer system used by air traffic controllers. If the air-traffic control system were to go on the blink, the results could be devastating. Ideally, the system should be repaired in minutes, if not seconds. Similarly, a stalled machine in a semiconductor fabrication plant could bring the entire manufacturing process to a standstill. Cohen explains that components for such critical products or services must be served by supply chains that differ dramatically from parts supply chains for non-critical products. Example: If a home hair dryer doesn't work, the worst result for the user would probably be a bad hair day.

Another key issue, according to Cohen, is determining the locations in the supply chain where a company should stock the parts. Should parts be stocked in a centralized fashion—say, a single warehouse or a small number of central warehouses? Or should the company have a far-flung network with multiple stocking points?

The answer, Cohen notes, depends on the criticality factor. In the case of computer systems for air traffic controllers, it makes sense to have critical components stocked over a wide network, so that plenty of points in the supply chain can back up one another when the parts are urgently needed. In contrast, a busted hair dryer could probably wait an extra day for parts to be shipped from a distant central warehouse or disposed of altogether by providing the customer with a replacement product.

Cohen, who has overseen research by several Ph.D. students over the years on such issues, developed many of these principles while studying parts availability in the automobile industry. Between 1985 and 1987, Cohen and his colleagues worked with General Motors to study the company's parts-supply chain network—at a time when the company was setting up Saturn as an independent firm. Cohen says that many of the recommendations that he and his colleagues made showed up as part of Saturn's service-support system.

Today Saturn has the highest off-the-shelf availability rate for parts of any car maker, according to *Parts Monitor*, a trade publication. In a paper published this year in the *Sloan Management Review*, Cohen and three colleagues—two of whom worked for GM and Saturn—point out that Saturn's performance was based on two key factors: Matching the company's supply-chain strategy to the criticality of its customers' needs, and involving dealers (or "retailers") in its supply-chain strategy.

Where is parts supply-chain management headed in the future? Cohen believes that with the coming of e-commerce, the field is moving toward a revolution. The main reason is that "technology has reached a point where large-scale optimization has become possible in real time," Cohen says. As a result of the Internet, it has now become possible for companies to create vast networks connecting their operations with those of their suppliers and customers. In the past, the hurdles to setting up such networks were so enormous that companies developed their own proprietary supply chains at enormous costs in time and money. As web-based technology takes off, however, the process of setting up such supply chains will become both faster and less expensive.

Cohen believes that it is now possible for him to commercialize some of his research. With a view to doing that, he last year launched MCA Solutions, an application service provider that offers supply chain services to clients. According to William C. Ross, the company's director of software engineering, the company's products give users a global bird's eye view of optimal inventory.

In a recent article written for the *Financial Times* Mastering Management series, Cohen and Vipul Agrawal, chief operating officer of MCA Solutions and a former professor at the Stern business school in New York City, explain how e-commerce will transform supply-chain management. Cohen and Agrawal believe that as companies' access to sources of supply increases as a result of web-based exchanges, "the dream of always providing the right product to the right customer at the right time and place and at the right price will very likely become a reality."

A good example of a company that is using the Internet to manage its supply chain is Dell Computer. According to Cohen and Agrawal, the company's web site allows customers to specify the configurations of their computers. This means that Dell can procure and assemble components at lower cost and with shorter lead times. Dell's supplier network can provide components to the company's assembly plant in Austin within hours of an order being placed. Dell's sales over the Internet now amount to more than $30 million a day.

Over time, more companies will migrate to such web-based supply-chain management systems. This may not happen as rapidly as some people hope, considering the setbacks this year to the Internet economy, but the supply-chain revolution is on its way— and there's no turning back.

6.

Thinking of Buying a
High-Tech Start-up? Read This First

Knowledge@Wharton, DATE TK

It is a familiar tale, especially in the volatile world of high technology. Managers in large, established firms look worriedly at the pace and variety of innovation in their industry and wonder how—if at all— they can keep up relying on internal R&D alone. In a garage a few streets away, a few creative geeks come together to start a company aimed at exploiting a new market niche. Fueled by entrepreneurial passion, long hours and coffee, the upstart firm sets a heady pace— and following some initial success, it gets an acquisition offer from a giant company in its industry.

Negotiations ensue. Offers and counter-offers are weighed. A deal is struck, and glowing press releases are issued. Six months or a year later, the most innovative people from the former start-up head for the door, leaving behind the husk of a once-thriving enterprise. All that is left is a disappointed debate over what went wrong.

Can companies avoid this scenario? Indeed they can, according to Phanish Puranam, a doctoral student at Wharton and soon-to-be faculty member at London Business School, who is studying mergers and acquisitions in high-tech industries with Harbir Singh, chair of Wharton's management department and Maurizio Zollo, who teaches management strategy at INSEAD.

Puranam, Singh and Zollo recently completed the first phase of a study exploring acquisitions by companies such as Cisco, Intel, Sun Microsystems and Hewlett-Packard. Their research shows that if high-tech companies want to succeed in their acquisition strategy, they must know what to change and not change after buying a start-up. "All integration decisions involve costs," says Puranam.

"Non-integration, too, however, involves costs. Successful acquirers must know how to manage both kinds of costs."

Puranam says the starting point is to recognize that acquisitions in the high-tech industry differ from those in other industries. "The single most important difference is that technology acquisitions are not about cost cutting," he notes. "Most traditional mergers and acquisitions are about gaining static efficiencies—you buy a company to make it work better. Technology mergers are about dynamic efficiencies. You don't ask how the acquisition will lower costs and improve your bottom line today; you ask how it will affect your ability to introduce new product lines that will improve your bottom line two or three years into the future." This is because in many high tech industries, innovations multiply over time. In other words, the software giant that buys a small start-up to gain access to a new product wants not just its current version, but also future ones. Acquirers usually buy innovation streams, not just one-shot innovations.

If this is true, it implies that managers need to handle high-tech mergers differently than they do those in other industries. One key variation: "Unlike a traditional merger where you take over a company and then fire people to lower costs, here the whole objective is to keep the product development teams intact," says Puranam. "In fact, you've bought the company because of its product development teams, and you've got to preserve their ability to be innovative."

How can that be done? That, explains Puranam, is where things get complicated. "Small firms don't work the same way that big ones do," he says. "An important difference involves the relationship between people's efforts and rewards." In a small company, an average person's work has a greater impact on the organization's performance than it would in a company with 30,000 employees. Small firms are able to nurture innovation because creative people get payoffs for their contributions, which are more visible. Once a large company takes over a small one, it risks disrupting this process. "Another difference involves the way in which people interact and communicate with one another in small organizations," says Puranam. "Smaller size and the absence of a strong hierarchy give start-up firms a unique culture and unique patterns of information flows, which might be essential to their innovativeness. The trick is to know what to change in the small firm and what not to change after the acquisition."

Cisco Systems, the Silicon Valley networking giant, has taken over some 70 small companies in recent years—and Puranam believes it has dealt with these issues better than most other high-tech behemoths. Puranam explains that when Cisco takes over a small company, it changes some things very rapidly. For example, it integrates the information-technology systems of the acquired firm into its own IT infrastructure. What it does not change, however, is the integrity of the R&D team. "It's unclear whether Cisco did this by design or by accident, but this has worked very well for Cisco," he says.

Cisco typically begins the integration process by taking apart the target firm: Technical units like the R&D team and the product management group are separated from support services such as sales and manufacturing. The latter are often redundant after the merger, since what Cisco brings to the table in any deal is its manufacturing and distribution capabilities as well as its reputation. Therefore, these activities get fully integrated into Cisco's corresponding functions. The R&D and product management teams, however, represent the heart of the small firm and the primary source of its value to Cisco. These groups are allowed to function as a quasi-autonomous business unit. In other words, the goose that lays the golden eggs doesn't get the ax; it gets its own nest.

"If we think about the extent of integration after an acquisition as the extent to which the target firm (or its sub-units) retain a distinctive administrative identity after acquisition, Cisco's approach may be described as one of low integration toward the R&D and product management groups and high integration for the rest of the firm," explains Puranam.

Other high-tech companies are increasingly beginning to follow this approach in their acquisitions. "With such an approach, if you were to speak to the product development team from a small firm after it has been acquired and ask its members what had changed for them after the acquisition, the answer is likely to be, 'Not much,'" says Puranam. "Most engineers continue to work with the same team-mates, report to the same technical boss, and work on the same projects." This approach minimizes the disruption to the team. Often, the team's high-powered incentives are preserved by linking the members' bonuses to team performance. Of course, it also helps if the stock options paid out are written on stocks that are shooting through the roof, as they were for Cisco until recently.

These steps allow acquirers to retain engineers from the target firm's product development teams, and even more importantly, to keep them productive. "I've looked at data showing new patents granted to engineers after Cisco has acquired their company," says Puranam. "This was part of our research that looked at the post-acquisition patenting behavior of inventors in target firms, and involved some 150 acquisitions by about 40 acquirers. Cisco was head and shoulders above other companies in terms of its performance along this dimension."

Cisco may have been able to use such an approach consistently because for the most part the company was buying stand-alone products to fill out its product portfolio. As long as the products developed by the target firm's teams were compatible with the rest of Cisco's product offerings and conformed to Cisco's design-for-manufacture process, there may have been little need to interfere with them. Puranam warns that such a hands-off approach may be less suitable when the R&D teams of the acquiring firm and the target firm are required to work very closely. In such cases, the benefits from integration may outweigh the disruption and incentive power loss.

High-tech acquirers that are less successful than Cisco in retaining creative expertise after a merger tend to err in two ways. "Mistakes are made at two ends of the spectrum," Puranam points out. "The first is doing no integration at all. You buy a company and keep it completely autonomous." This might initially seem to be a good idea. It certainly is popular among people from the target company, since they do not feel pressured by the acquiring organization. "The question to ask is, why did the large company acquire the small one if it did not mean to touch it at all," says Puranam. "Why couldn't it have entered into an alliance or a joint venture or even bought a minority stake? What is the point in paying more money and taking on more risk by acquiring the company if you do not intend to extract value?"

The second error is to aim at complete integration and blend the small firm seamlessly with the large one. This, also, might initially seem to work because it allows the acquiring company to eliminate redundancies and avoid problems that arise from having to manage administrative diversity. "But over time you realize that the very things that made the small firm valuable—especially its innovativeness—have gone," says Puranam. "Of course, while we can point out that generic advice to "integrate fully" or "keep your hands off" are both incorrect, and that intermediate levels of integration may often be appropriate, what needs to be done in a given acquisition depends on the specifics of the deal."

It is also true that in cases where the R&D team leaves after a takeover, the reason may not always be disruption and loss in incentive power. A key factor may be that the top management team in the small firm, which often owns a significant amount of stock in their firm, may want to cash out and so no longer have an incentive to stay around and be productive. Puranam argues that the first step toward solving this problem is to ask if the acquirer wants the top management team to stay after the acquisition. "Sometimes you may want both the top management team and the engineers; at other times, you may want just the engineers and not the top management team," he says.

What the acquiring company does depends on its goals for the acquisition. "If your goal is to create completely new product lines in the future, then you should hang on to the entrepreneurs and the top management team," says Puranam. "These people will help you make it happen." Companies like Sun Microsystems and Intel are trying to do this by turning founders of companies they have acquired into so-called intrapreneurs or entrepreneurs in residence. "Large companies have an internal corporate ventures unit. Entrepreneurs and their top managers are recognized as people who are good at championing and developing new ideas. They may not be as good at managing day-to-day operations. So you might want to move them into the corporate ventures unit where they continue to develop new ventures."

In contrast, if the large company's goal for the merger is to acquire just one new product and the ability to make successive innovations on that product alone, it does not need the entrepreneur or top managers. In January 1996, when Microsoft bought Vermeer Technologies, the Massachussetts-based firm that developed FrontPage, the popular web-page authoring software, it took this approach. "Vermeer's top management left within a year, but Microsoft did not mind because it was interested mainly in the software developers," says Puranam. "Microsoft made one big change; it moved everyone to Seattle. This is standard policy at Microsoft —because it believes that monitoring and information sharing across groups are easier when everyone is in the same location. But after the Vermeer engineers went to Seattle,

Microsoft let them work in their old teams and made no attempt to split them up." FrontPage has remained a successful application under Microsoft's mantle, Puranam adds.

Puranam says that his research with Singh and Zollo points to three overall conclusions:

1. **All integration decisions involve tradeoffs.** If an acquiring company integrates the target company too little or too much into its existing structure, it will lose value. Finding the right balance is therefore crucial.

2. **All integration decisions involve costs.** Integration efforts take up managerial time, and where layoffs are involved, they also involve severance and other costs. While this is usually understood, an issue that is often overlooked is that non-integration also involves costs. "You can get a demotivating effect if employees in the acquiring firm begin to question their value because their counterparts in the target firm are treated differently (and perhaps better)," says Puranam. "Such non-integration costs are hard to capture on a balance sheet, but they are real and hurt productivity."

3. **Successful high-tech acquirers have capabilities that let them cut both integration and non-integration costs.** Reducing integration costs is often a matter of experience. Companies that do a lot of acquisitions and keep learning from the process—as Hewlett Packard or Intel have done—are able to streamline their acquisition capability and become very good at it. Among financial firms, Bank One has gained lots of expertise at mergers not only by doing several of them, but also by putting in place a process to capture and codify the knowledge obtained through these experiences.

Non-integration costs, though, are rarely under managerial control. These have much more to do with an organization's history and culture. "If you are a large decentralized firm with great diversity in pay and benefits, if you acquire a small company and maintain it on a different incentive scheme no one may care. That is the norm in your firm," says Puranam. "On the other hand, if you have fairly homogeneous pay, benefits and autonomy for a given level across the organization, if you acquire a firm whose people are then treated differently than the rest, the word will get around. This is rarely something that individual decision makers can control when they are looking at an acquisition."

This last factor, notes Puranam, points to an interesting result. Over integration is often blamed when people from an acquired start-up leave, but the critics may not realize that the company is simply trying to avoid non-integration costs. "The executives in the big company aren't crazy," he says. "This may just be the cost of doing business in their industry. Not integrating the start-up into its larger organization may be more expensive than integrating it." Understanding this tradeoff may help save much heartache later for both people in the target firm and those who are acquiring it.

7.

"It is Absolutely Critical in a Merger to Quickly Establish Unambiguous Lines of Responsibility"

Knowledge@Wharton, March 29, 2000

Deutsche Bank is merging its way to growth. Headquartered in Frankfurt, it has 90,000 employees and nearly 7 million customers in more than 60 nations. On March 9 the bank announced a $30 billion merger agreement with Dresdner Bank; the two companies are scheduled to merge before the end of the year. This deal follows its acquisition last year of Bankers Trust for $10.1 billion. This makes Deutsche Bank one of the world's largest financial institutions.

What challenges do organizations face as they try to make such mega-mergers work? What is involved in managing organizations across cultural boundaries? Michael Useem, director of the Wharton School's Center for Leadership and Change Management, discussed these questions with John Ross, president and CEO of Deutsche Bank's American operations.

Useem: Before becoming president and chief executive officer of Deutsche Bank Americas in mid-1999 you served as CEO of Deutsche Bank Group Asia Pacific. What were the one or two biggest challenges in running a German bank in the Asian region?

Ross: The challenges in that part of the world had nothing to do with our being a German bank. At that time the challenge was that Asia was in a crisis. Secondly, we were trying to go from being an old-line commercial bank to a modern investment bank. As a result, not only were our clients wondering whether we were going to do what other banks were doing—which was to withdraw capital from the region—but we also had internal staff members wondering whether they would keep their jobs. This was, first, because of the Asian crisis; and second, because we were looking for a different business model. Eventually things worked out quite successfully for us, primarily because change is easier to implement in a crisis than when things are going spectacularly well.

We made a policy decision that we were going to grow in Asia rather than contract. Our clients, both government and corporate, responded very well to this decision. We were able to do things that in the normal course of events would have taken much longer. With Asians it typically takes a longer time to establish relationships, than in the West, but in a crisis, you can make things happen faster.

Our strategy of expanding in Asia and building an investment bank was very well received by our staff and by clients. The staff members came to realize that they did have the requisite job skills. We simplified the management structure and made our business objectives and organizational structure known clearly. I went to Asia at the start of March 1998 and we were completely reorganized by June. We stuck to a clear, simple strategy and conveyed it to our clients, reinforced it with the staff, and this turned out to be a very effective approach. Being a German bank made no difference.

Useem: Since Deutsche Bank's acquisition of Bankers Trust in June 1999, you have been at the forefront of integrating two very different banking cultures. Could you describe the most important cultural differences between the two banks and what you have done to overcome them?

Ross: One of the great challenges we had in the merger was convincing people that the cultures were not all that different. Yes, it is true that Deutsche Bank is headquartered in Germany. It is also true that Deutsche Bank was for years seen as a commercial bank and Bankers Trust as a wholesale bank. And obviously, Bankers Trust is headquartered in New York City, so there must be cultural differences between the two. That was the simple assumption.

The fact, however, is that before the change of control, two of Deutsche Bank's five main divisions were run by non-Germans, and approximately 35% to 40% of the staff of Deutsche Bank were non-German. The investment bank—inside Deutsche Bank we call the investment bank Global Corporates and Institutions (GCI)—is one of the five main business divisions. That division, as it turned out, is predominantly run by Americans. The bulk of the staff inside GCI are either American or British. The bulk of the income that was made at Bankers Trust was made by their wholesale banking business lines, and so it was basically Americans talking to Americans. There was really very little culture clash.

Deutsche Bank also recognized that it is absolutely critical in a merger to quickly establish unambiguous lines of responsibility and make senior executive decisions as rapidly as possible. Such decisions should also be implemented as soon as possible. We did that with Bankers Trust, so that there was no confusion about who was running what, who was responsible for what, and what was the game-plan and strategy going forward.

We had a period of almost six months from the date of the merger agreement to the change of control date. Therefore, on the actual day when the change of control occurred, June 4, 1999, it wasn't a sudden change. It was the continuation of a strategy and chain of command that had already been well communicated during the prior four months.

Useem: You referred to the importance of making prompt executive decisions. When you hire or promote a senior manager at the bank, what do you look for in the person's record and style to know if the individual will be effective in working, managing, and leading across cultural and national boundaries?

Ross: Ideally we look for market leadership in the particular product line the individual is working in. Secondly, we want to know if the person is a good communicator and is innovative. Deutsche Bank espouses five values: Client focus, performance, innovation, teamwork and trust. We look for all these values in our staff, whether they are in junior or senior management. We look to see whether prospective candidates fit those values. Where the candidates come from—i.e., their nationality—is irrelevant.

One fact that pleasantly surprised executives from Bankers Trust after the acquisition was that we are probably the most multinational of any financial services firms in the world. When you look at the bank's executive committee, you will see that close to 40% of the members are non-German. I don't think any of our competitors can state that that large a percentage of their executive committee is made up of people whose citizenship is not that of the firm's country of incorporation. This is not particularly well understood by people globally before they consider joining Deutsche Bank, but it is a very strong argument for us when we do speak to them and demonstrate that it is the case. Newspapers have now started picking up on this as well.

Useem: The announcement on March 9 that Deutsche Bank and Dresdner bank will join to form one of the world's largest banks presents a new set of challenges for managing cultural differences. From your experience in overseeing Deutsche Bank's integration of Bankers Trust, what advice would you have for consolidating your merger with Dresdner?

Ross: We are doing the same thing that we did in the case of Bankers Trust, which is to early on make decisions about who is doing what, who is responsible for what, and make sure that those people are able to communicate with their own management teams. This ensures that on the change-of-control date there is no ambiguity or loss of momentum otherwise, you lose revenues; clients tend to take their business to the competition until you've sorted out your management problems; you get bad press; and staff are agitated and tend to focus on their own personal concerns.

One of the biggest problems in mergers arises out of lack of decision making early on. If there is lack of clarity with regard to reporting lines, responsibilities, strategy, and so on, a merger that looks great on paper can turn out to be problematic. Another mistake that I have seen some companies make is that they try to be 100% correct in every decision they make before change of control. You can be 85% or better correct—and often that is good enough. You may make mistakes, but if you are flexible you can correct them later.

Useem: Drawing on your service with Deutsche Bank's operations in both Asia and the Americas, what are the most important qualities required for leading the growth of global banking?

Ross: You have to believe in the premise that we live in a global environment. Therefore, working globally, you need to be flexible enough to understand and be considerate of other cultures because you are trying to do business with those cultures. If you work for an American firm, you may find that outside the U.S. American managers may not always be the best choice. What should clearly count is product knowledge and the five values I mentioned before. Managers should espouse those values and demonstrate them. If you are an American firm, leaving the impression in the market that only Americans can get ahead will limit you in terms of the talent pool you can draw from. This is also true of German firms. We have made it clear globally that you don't have to be German to get ahead inside Deutsche Bank.

8.

How Virtual Communities Enhance Knowledge

Knowledge@Wharton, March 21, 2000

Technology has long redefined notions of distance. For past generations, the telephone, the radio and the television set were tools that bridged vast geographic spaces. Today the Internet is taking this phenomenon further—and dramatically so. As more people join e-mail lists, hobnob in chat rooms and participate in online events, virtual communities have emerged—both within companies and on the Internet—that let people communicate in ways and at speeds that were unimaginable in the past.

What implications do virtual communities have for companies? Can they help global organizations share knowledge and best practices? What special challenges do they face in issues like establishing trust and maintaining control?

Knowledge@Wharton discussed these questions and more with Bruce Kogut, co-director of the Reginald H. Jones Center for Management Policy, Strategy and Organization, and Laurence Prusak, executive director of the IBM Institute for Knowledge Management.

The IBM Institute of Knowledge Management, the Reginald H. Jones Center of the Wharton School and the Xerox Palo Alto Research Center (PARC) will discuss these issues in greater detail at a conference about Virtual Communities and the Internet on April 7 in Philadelphia.

Knowledge@Wharton: What makes for a strong virtual community?

Prusak: I'm not sure that there is such a thing as a virtual community. The jury is out that you can actually have a virtual community without some overriding, compelling reason for people to act in a "community" way with one another. What do I mean by that? Obviously parents of ill children get together very often virtually on websites. They exchange information, tips for help, and so forth. Is that a community? I suppose so—in the widest definition of the word. But those people have an absolute, compelling need to share information.

But the word community is now being applied to almost everything. The British social scientist Raymond Williams once said that community is the only word in English that has no negative connotations. Everyone likes to use the word community to mean all sorts of things. So I'm not sure about virtual communities. I'm curious to see what we learn in five years.

In the business world, if people have come together because they have been given a task or they have been driven by a hard manager—for example, because they have to get a new product out by a certain day—they might come together to exchange information over the Internet. They may be motivated either by fear or the desire to bring about some sort of collective outcome. Is that a community? I'm not so sure. In my perspective, communities are driven by some sort of altruism, in which people are acting without evident self-interest. I don't see that happening too much in business. Maybe it does happen, but you see it a lot less.

Kogut: A community is, first of all, a place where there is value in the members and in the membership. This is a radical challenge to the sales concept that a firm sells to a consumer. Now, in part, the customers as members provide a service to each other in serving themselves. A firm owns and invests in the franchise for this community. At the same time, the franchise is a gift from members that has to be always renewed.

Knowledge@Wharton: In the online world, where people don't see one another, how can communities resolve issues of trust, identity and anonymity?

Kogut: Often, these issues are not resolved and there is no reason to resolve them! The very attraction of some communities is that members can play with their identities. An interesting issue is when should a virtual identity be pierced? Of course, this happens somewhere in the interface at the point of sale. But it also comes up when members want to have reliable information and this means reputations must be established and known. Here such sites as Amazon and E-bay have been very innovative in permitting reputations to be established despite anonymous identities.

Prusak: I don't think virtual communities can resolve these issues. People have to get together in the real world. Three organizations I know are studying this: AT&T, Procter & Gamble and the U.S. army. At different levels, they have all studied how much so-called face time you need for a community to have coherence. They all felt that people have to actually meet, either once a month or every other month or some such number. Without that, you get entropy. You lose your edge, and passion cannot be transmitted. Things also get ragged; it's like an orchestra being conducted without a conductor. I have yet to hear about a "community" that has never met and still has coherence. Maybe some religious communities might exist, which, like the parents of sick children, may be highly motivated. I can imagine that. But in business, I don't think that's possible. People have to meet to transmit passion.

Knowledge@Wharton: Virtual communities also face issues of netiquette and what is called virtual self government. How can control be exercised in virtual communities?

Kogut: This is a very tough issue. Lauwrence Lessig's book *Code* is very helpful in showing that the software code of any community establishes a certain constitution. I think he is right in dispelling us of the notion that the virtual community is the wild west of no government and no rules. There are strong incentives for a firm to intervene because it understands that its franchise is valuable. But often the tendency is for the firm to try to help members self-govern rather than strong-arm a solution. It does this by working with the community and also putting in technology that allows members to establish "filters" and to be able to organize in sub-communities.

Prusak: This is very interesting. I'm in IBM, and I get a lot of messages. Norms seem to get established in terms of answering e-mail, for example, of who answers whom in what way. These norms are different if you are all in the same building. I have a nice suite of offices in Lotus, but there are only 15 of us and of course I answer e-mail from the 14 people who work with me here. If I were in a large facility, I would be talking to a lot more people. As it is, some of them send me long e-mails that I can barely understand, and I just ignore them. One of the norms that gets established is that you don't have to respond, which you would if you were co-located.

Whether that is good or bad for business is an interesting issue. It may make people more efficient, or they may miss opportunities. Maybe I help people less than I could. But this question is worth looking at and doing research on.

Exercising control in a virtual community would be very difficult. I haven't encountered a situation that requires control in the virtual world, but I can easily imagine that. I don't think there is much that one could do, except perhaps isolate, exile or ostracize the person.

Knowledge@Wharton: What is the relationship between virtual communities and the real world? What implications does this have for business?

Prusak: The word community is being bandied about now for the reason that Raymond Williams said: It's a warm, happy, fuzzy word. From my perspective, any organization that has small, tightly integrated networks could be called communities. Usually these are focused on a practice. These practices have their own language, vocabulary, repertoire, and artifacts—and these are all real things. Organizations can make these networks more efficient by giving them resources, money, technology, time and space.

The World Bank has taken this as far as any group in the world. It has 122 communities or networks—they call them thematic groups—of people who are globally dispersed, but share a passion around rural road building, or indigenous peoples, or rural portfolio improvement, forestry, or issues like that. The groups are diverse and are spread around the world, but they share information and help each other. The World Bank has really been rebuilt around these groups, which have leaders, people, technology and money. They even publish documents. [Wharton economist] Sid Winter asked a question in one of his articles: Where is the knowledge in an organization? Well, the knowledge of the World Bank is in these groups.

Kogut: As an academic, I never believed that strongly in this difference in any event. You know, a good educational environment is one that not only teaches about the actual world, but also about possible worlds. The virtual is a real world, but there are many realities from which to choose. This is the fundamental starting point or else we will never understand the importance of fantasy, of interaction, of the thrill of anonymous behavior. At the same time, the value of many virtual communities is their reality. They improve the delivery of medical services, for example, by allowing patients to converse. If reality is improved information and understanding, the virtual communities provide a preferred reality over what was possible before.

Knowledge@Wharton: Is a company's Internet strategy related to the building of virtual communities? What are the principal challenges in this regard?

Kogut: What we know about successful Internet strategies is that the fundamental concept has to be customer satisfaction. It is not the portal, not the auction, it is the customer. How this satisfaction will be provided, of course, differs by community.

Prusak: The Internet provides an infrastructure for communication. It's better than a phone line, and easier than a fax in some ways. I use the Internet as a more interesting and richer form of communication than is possible over telephone lines. But the Internet does not create altruism or a feeling that people should help one another. A researcher at MIT has written a very interesting book about predictions made after the telephone was invented. As commercial telephony grew, all sorts of predictions were made about how it would change society and human behavior. Not one of them came true. Not one. The biggest prediction, and the most common, was that there wouldn't be wars any more if people could talk directly to one another. Now there's a lot of that kind of stuff about the Internet too. The web certainly creates new distribution channels and new ways of selling stuff, but frankly, if we live in a materialist and individualistic culture, it is still going to be materialist and individualistic.

As for the relation between a company's Internet strategy and virtual communities, I believe that the richer the tools that are available to people, the more likely it is that they will self-organize in networks. If you give people good tools, they will find each other. The World Bank did not create its thematic groups; they were there. The bank gave them money, time and technology— but those people were there. If you love rural road building, and other people do, you will get together. Karl Marx wrote about classes being "in themselves" and "for themselves." This is like that. These people existed, just not in each other's consciousness. The Internet can help them connect and find one another.

Knowledge@Wharton: How can virtual communities facilitate the sharing of knowledge and best practices?

Prusak: I tend to think, as do many others, that knowledge is sticky, local and contextual. Very little can be codified and put in a form that a machine can transmit. Some knowledge can be codified and transmitted, but a lot cannot. Try learning to hit a baseball just by reading words. It's almost impossible. Certainly a better thing would be to see a movie of someone hitting a baseball.

There's a lot you cannot transmit with just words. You may be able to do recipes or certain types of prototypes, but real knowledge—how to be a blacksmith, how to hang a door on a car on an assembly line, how a chemist at a big R&D site makes big intuitive leaps—I don't think technology plays a big role in developing such knowledge.

At IBM we constantly try to build and rebuild best-practice databases, and I know all the consulting firms try to do that, but these are worth very little. People learn by going out with people who know how to do things and watching how they do it.

Some companies have a purely technological approach to knowledge sharing. They create document repositories and they believe that that equals knowledge transfer. I know how to do something; I write it up, and it goes into a Lotus database; then someone can read it. Such an approach is almost worthless—not totally so, but almost. If I want to read an article you wrote, I may be able to read it in a database. But if I want to know how to become a chemist, or to think like a chemist or act in a lab, I cannot do that by searching a database.

Some companies are getting interested in the apprenticeship model, which is a much better way of transferring knowledge. This involves insisting that projects be staffed in a way that younger people have a chance to work with older people. The Big Five firms try to do this, but they are often so driven by greed that the older partner sells the work but then passes it on to a lot of junior people. I think some consulting firms are trying the apprenticeship model, and more companies should. The Germans and the Japanese built the No. 2 and No. 3 economies in the world using this model of sharing knowledge through moving people around as apprentices. It's a very complex issue.

Kogut: I am glad you asked this question, because it allows me to correct the impression that communities only serve final customers. Communities are rapidly developing in the area of business-to-business markets. This is obvious for the auctions used for material products. Intranet communities offer another promising area of development. Certainly we as educators are thinking a lot about virtual learning communities among our students, how to develop them, how to support them. In business, firms such as BP-Amoco have been taking an active role in supporting the sharing of practices by IT-enabled infrastructures that are yet sensitive to the human dimension.

Knowledge@Wharton: How do you see the future of virtual communities?

Kogut: The idea of loyal customers has always been there. The French have an expression that is hard to translate and that is a strategy to 'loyalize' the customer. A virtual community does this by improving the perceived value of products and services and also providing a satisfaction in the act of buying.

Prusak: I am a great believer in the technology not of words and numbers, but of sight, smell and sound. As the PC evolves, and you get real-time communication and face-to-face discussions over long distances, things will get better. The closer you get to two people sitting down and having a chat, the closer you get to knowledge transmission and community building.

9.

Mercenaries vs. Missionaries: John Doerr Sees Two Kinds of Internet Entrepreneurs

Knowledge@Wharton, April 13, 2000

John Doerr, whom Fortune magazine once described as America's "only celebrity venture capitalist," has often said that the personal computer industry's growth from zero to $100 billion in 10 years was "the greatest legal accumulation of wealth in history." Now he has something to add about the Internet revolution: It has dwarfed the PC revolution by going from zero to $400 billion in five years. "There are waves," says Doerr, "and then there is a tsunami."

That tsunami—which has ushered in a new economy symbolized by Silicon Valley, where unemployment is minus 3% and incomes of every segment of society are rising—has drawn much of its might from the activities of people like Doerr. During the past two decades he and his partners at Kleiner Perkins Caufield & Byers, the best-known venture capital firm in Silicon Valley and arguably the U.S., have financed—and often helped build—such firms as Compaq, Netscape, Lotus, Sun Microsystems and Amazon, among others. If the best way to predict the future is to invent it, "the second-best way is to finance it," says Doerr. He should know: Kleiner Perkins has so far invested $1.3 billion in 250 technology ventures, which have created 192,000 jobs, achieved $73 billion in sales and a market value of nearly half a trillion dollars.

Such staggering wealth creation, however, is not the most important thing about Silicon Valley, says Doerr, who was the keynote speaker on March 31 at a conference organized by Wharton in San Francisco, and spoke on topics ranging from emerging trends in the new economy to the crisis in education. The most important fact about Silicon Valley—which Doerr describes as "a state of mind" that also exists in some other areas in the U.S.—is that it has unleashed the power of the entrepreneur. "Entrepreneurs are America's new heroes," says Doerr. "They have been provocateurs, risk-takers and innovators. They have moved from land to industrial assets to ideas. They are now entering fields of social entrepreneurship, such as education. This is the latest social change in history."

The foundations of the new economy, notes Doerr, rest on four pillars: The silicon chip, the PC, the Internet and genomics. The new economy, he adds, threatens the old economy in fundamental ways. "The old economy was about people acquiring a single skill for life; the new economy is about life-long learning," says Doerr. "The old economy was about monopolies; the new economy is about competition. The old economy was about job preservation; the new economy is about job creation. The old economy was about wages; the new economy is about ownership. The old economy got its value from plant equipment; the new economy gets its value from intellectual property. The old economy was like sumo wrestling; the new one is like the 100-meter dash; the old economy emphasized standardization; the new one stresses choice. The old economy sued; the new economy invests."

As the new economy grows, a battle is raging for its soul. The combatants are those whose aim is to build great companies to provide long-term value, versus those who want to create companies that can be sold for a quick profit. Citing a recent cover story in Fast Company magazine, Doerr points out that the fight is between those who want to build companies to last and those who want to build them to flip.

Five factors distinguish truly great ventures, in Doerr's view. They are led by missionaries, not mercenaries; they have top-notch, passionate leadership; they operate in large, rapidly-growing and underserved markets; they have reasonable levels of financing; and most importantly, they work with a sense of urgency. "This is a period of extreme time famine," says Doerr. "Time is the most precious resource for the 10th of the planet that is ready for the new economy."

What distinguishes companies led by mercenaries from those led by missionaries? While the two might seem similar at first glance, they are in fact very different, Doerr points out. "Mercenaries are driven by paranoia; missionaries are driven by passion," he says. "Mercenaries think opportunistically; missionaries think strategically. Mercenaries go for the sprint; missionaries go for the marathon. Mercenaries focus on their competitors and financial statements; missionaries focus on their customers and value statements. Mercenaries are bosses of wolf packs; missionaries are mentors or coaches of teams. Mercenaries worry about entitlements; missionaries are obsessed with making a contribution. Mercenaries are motivated by the lust for making money; missionaries, while recognizing the importance of money, are fundamentally driven by the desire to make meaning."

Doerr believes that as the new economy develops, several trends are emerging. Among his forecasts for the future:

- IP, or internet protocol, will be as important as the car or television.

- The web will become the standard communications platform in healthcare.

- Charter schools, and educational portals for the home and school, will transform education.

- Bandwidth will be crucial.

- Despite current skepticism about business-to-consumer e-commerce, it will remain a big trend, as will business-to-business e-commerce.

- Wireless information appliances will be big in the future. "That's how a billion Chinese will get onto the Internet," Doerr says.

- Genomics will be "fabulous" after 2005, as the human genome is fully mapped.

Doerr also predicts that the Internet will evolve into what he calls "the Evernet," which is "always on, high speed, ubiquitous and available in multiple formats." These formats will include a "voiceweb" for voice communications, a "handweb" for hand-held devices, a "PC web" for PCs, a "videoweb" for video and an "e-web" in which machines will communicate with machines. These changes will consolidate the foundations of the new economy.

If the new economy faces one significant challenge, according to Doerr, it is that today's generation of children is being inadequately prepared to run it in the future. "While higher education is in good shape, primary education is in a crisis," Doerr says. The problem isn't lack of money; California alone spends $35 billion a year on education. The problem isn't even teachers, many of whom are highly dedicated. The problem is the system. "Many kids are promoted even if they can't pass tests," he observes. The result: 42 million Americans cannot read, and 60 million, despite an eighth grade education, have serious problems with reading and algebra. If this situation persists, children will be unable to develop the symbolic reasoning skills they will need to work in the new economy.

How can the crisis in education be tackled? The solution is not to hook up more PCs in classrooms, says Doerr. "Schools need smaller class sizes and a longer school day and year. They also need teachers who are given enough time and incentives to excel." Doerr points out that innovation, accountability, choice, competition, leadership and parental involvement will be required to overcome the crisis in education. One positive sign, he says, is that social entrepreneurs have begun to get involved in attacking the crisis. Among them: organizations and foundations with web sites such as www.successforall.net, www.letsfixourschools.com, and www.publicschools.org.

"Figure out a way to get involved," Doerr says. "Make a difference in a way that works for you."

10.

What Xerox Should Copy, and Not Copy, from Its Past

Knowledge@Wharton, October 25, 2000

Flashback to 1982: Xerox is under siege. Japanese rivals such as Canon, Minolta and Ricoh have made devastating inroads into the company's core market, and observers are starting to wonder whether the Stamford, Conn.-based giant, whose name is synonymous with photocopying, can survive. David T. Kearns, Xerox's CEO, however, is out to disprove the pessimists. Convinced that the copier market has more life left than the skeptics think, he drives Xerox to focus on bettering the quality of its products, technology and after-sales service. Six relentless years later, the company bounces back. The story of Xerox's turnaround becomes a case study for aspiring MBAs.

Fast forward to 2000: Xerox, again, is under siege, and questions are being raised about its ability to survive. This time, though, it isn't just competitors that are nipping at Xerox's heels. Revenues—$19.2 billion in 1999—are flat; earnings are plunging; and the company has been caught in such a severe cash crunch that its ability to sell commercial paper to pay its bills has been impaired. The firing of CEO Richard Thoman, a former IBM executive, in May and his replacement by Paul Allaire, who led Xerox through most of the 1990s, has done little to help. The price of Xerox shares, which traded for $64 in May 1999, has dropped to its lowest level in years. The stock closed on October 24 at a little more than $8.

The big question before Xerox today is whether it can make history repeat itself. Allaire and Anne M. Mulcahey, who was named president following Thoman's departure, believe it can. On October 24, while announcing a third-quarter loss of 20 cents a share, they also announced a turnaround program that included cutting $1 billion in costs and raising between $2 billion and $4 billion through the sale of assets. Among other steps, Allaire says, Xerox plans to sell its China operations, a part of its ownership in Fuji Xerox (a subsidiary in Japan that serves much of Asia) and other Xerox concerns. In addition, Xerox is looking into a possible joint venture with "noncompetitive partners" for its legendary Palo Alto Research Center.

Allaire hopes that the combination of these steps will toss Xerox the lifeline it needs at this critical juncture and help the company rebound—just as it has often done in the past. "This will sharpen our competitive edge, deliver the superior products and services that our customers require, and generate the value that our credit providers and shareholders require," he says.

Others, however, are less gung-ho about Xerox's prospects. Some experts, including Wharton faculty, point out that while the company undoubtedly has great strengths—including an exceptionally strong track record at innovation and a tradition of resilience—its ability to sustain itself will depend on whether Xerox can copy—and not copy—fundamental lessons from its past and forge a new strategy for the future.

One mistake that these experts urge Xerox not to copy is that of developing innovative technologies that other companies eventually turn into big winners. Bruce Kogut, co-director of Wharton's Reginald H. Jones Center for Management Policy, Strategy and Organization, argues that Xerox has tended to do this in the past. "The company developed amazing technologies—the laser printer, the graphical user interface for personal computers, the computer mouse—but it couldn't commercialize them," Kogut says. "The feeling at Xerox was that all these innovations would go into the ecology of Silicon Valley, and then return to the company. But in the meanwhile, other companies captured value from Xerox's innovations."

The story of how Xerox failed to capture value from its creation of the personal computer and its graphical user interface is now well known—and Douglas Smith and Robert Alexander tell it at length in their book, *"Fumbling the Future: How Xerox Invented, Then Ignored, the First Personal Computer."* Writer Owen Linzmayer recounts a part of that story in his recent book, *"Apple Confidential: The Real Story of Apple Computer."*

In November 1979 Apple co-founder Steve Jobs visited the Xerox PARC labs with some engineers from Apple. When Jobs saw the software that Xerox researchers had developed—with its moveable overlapping windows and pop-up menus—he reportedly began to jump around, shouting: "Why aren't you doing anything with this? This is the greatest thing! This is revolutionary!" These features later became part of Apple's successful line of MacIntosh computers, as they are today of Microsoft's Windows software. (Xerox did sue Apple over the graphical user interface in the mid 1980s, but the lawsuit went nowhere.)

Mark B. Myers, former senior vice president of research and technology at Xerox, and now a senior fellow at Wharton's Emerging Technologies Management Research Program and the SEI Center for Advanced Management Research, finds another missed opportunity more galling. "In fairness to Xerox, it had just introduced xerography around 1960, and it was going through an extraordinary innovative explosion during the 1970s," he says. "The company was not prepared then for another major revolution—the client-server paradigm was larger than any company that existed at that time could manage. My own regret, however, is that although Xerox invented laser printing—a technology close to its birthright—Hewlett-Packard eventually ended up dominating that market. It was Xerox's most difficult loss of opportunity."

Why did Xerox fail to capitalize on its invention of the laser printer? One factor, explains Myers, is that the company was a victim of its own success. The company had traditionally relied on direct sales by its own sales force, which was an extremely profitable undertaking. The laser printing products, however, had to be marketed through computer superstores and other sales channels, which squeezed the profit margins in that business. "Xerox focused on businesses that had extremely high profit margins, rather than those that had rapid turns characteristic of low-margin businesses," he says. The result, however, was that Xerox all but abandoned the laser-printer field to rivals like Hewlett-Packard until it was too late.

The enormous profitability of Xerox's core business also hampered the company's ability to develop peripheral opportunities. During the 1960s and early 1970s, Xerox had a virtual monopoly on its copying technology, protected by its patents. The company saw a period of phenomenal expansion during those years, growing by some estimates at a compounded annual rate of more than 40%. That success, however, dampened the company's motivation to develop other innovations.

Xerox eventually was forced to give up its exclusive monopoly on xerography and had to license its technology to rivals. That, in part, created the competitive pressures from Japanese firms like Canon, Minolta and Ricoh, which prompted the counter-attack led by Kearns during the 1980s. Kearns also believed that Xerox would have to move its products from an analog to a digital base. Allaire, who succeeded Kearns as CEO in 1990, continued to develop Xerox along digital lines during most of the 1990s. Among other things, he pulled Xerox out of financial businesses such as insurance to focus on digital technology. Xerox's goal, he believed, should be to become a company that helped clients organize all their documents—digital as well as physical.

While these were steps in the right direction, they did not protect Xerox against serious errors. The current crisis has developed rapidly during the past two years. A big part of the problem was that the company mandated a sales force and billing systems reorganization with disastrous results. Although most observers blame this initiative on Thoman, who succeeded Allaire as CEO in 1999, Allaire cannot entirely escape responsibility because he was the company chairman when it was introduced. Under the new rules, the sales force was to be organized along industry lines rather than geographic ones, so that each sales person could sell all of Xerox's products and services to the same client.

George Day, director of Wharton's Emerging Technologies Research Management Program, points out that while the move was "directionally correct, its execution was appalling." The sales force reorganization undermined Xerox's customer relationships, and Thoman was criticized for creating a disruptive situation. To make matters worse, "the new billing system could not support these changes, and that fouled up the billing process," says Day. "Customers stopped paying their bills, and then cash flow problems began to appear. That is why Thoman lost his job. He was aggressive and quick to make decisions, but he did not have the support of key members within the company."

Gabriel Szulanksi, who teaches management at Wharton, says Xerox got into trouble with its reorganization efforts because it tried to force through changes without adequate preparation. "Even before Thoman became the CEO, he toured Europe and saw some innovative sales practices at units like Rank Xerox," he explains. While these were clearly efficient practices within their original context, Thoman went too far in believing that these best practices could be standardized and mandated throughout the organization without first preparing people for them. "Xerox offers a wonderful example of taking knowledge management in too big a dose," Szulanski says. "The sales force reorganization killed a capability that Xerox had. When you do that, you fall into the same trap that the advocates of business process re-engineering did in the past. It just becomes another good reason to fire people."

While Xerox struggled with these problems—which also contributed to a high staff turnover rate as people left to pursue other opportunities—it was slammed by intense competition from rivals. At the lower end of its product range, companies like Canon and Ricoh continued to hound Xerox, while at the higher end, rivals such as Heidelberger Druckmaschinen AG, a German firm, began to make forays into Xerox's market. "These moves can cause long-term damage to Xerox," says Day. "Its customer relationships are being taken over by competitors."

Will the reorganization plan that Allaire announced on Oct. 24 succeed in turning the tide? Day, for one, has his doubts. "Many of these steps have the appearance of having been in the works for some time," he says. Others point out that it is difficult to assess their impact until more details are known. For example, Xerox has a crucial relationship with Fuji through its Fuji Xerox venture in

Japan. If the company sells a part of its stake in this venture, it will take some time to determine how that will affect Xerox's operations in Asia. The sale of the Chinese subsidiary, too, could be a quick fix in the short-run, but Xerox's ability to raise cash will depend upon how much more investment in that subsidiary will be needed in the future. Overall, it is unclear what impact the proposed reorganization will have. Xerox may need to do more to reduce its $18 billion in debt and increase its profitability.

Myers points out that the success of the reorganization plan depends on one more crucial issue: Xerox's ability to figure out how to become profitable in a business that is rapidly changing. Thanks to the continuing commoditization of copying and printing technology, as well as pressure from competitors, Xerox faces a future in which its profit margins will potentially be lower than they have been in the past. "Xerox knows how to be profitable in a high-margin business," says Myers. "The question is, can the company become profitable in a low-margin business?"

If there is one lesson from its past that Xerox should copy, however, that is its tenacity in bouncing back from looming disaster. Asks Szulanski: "Would I buy Xerox stock today? I'm tempted…because the company has promising technologies and some very smart people. The company is just in a fragile position today." Adds Kogut: "Xerox has seen adversity before and rebounded, while also preserving its social community by avoiding layoffs. The company has a strong internal culture that may allow it over time to respond effectively." Myers, too, is hopeful. "Xerox's story has never been tranquil," he says, "but it has always been an innovative company."

That history of innovation might yet work in Allaire's favor as he and his fellow executives try to turn things around at Xerox. If they succeed, they could provide future MBA students with yet one more case study to peruse.

11.
Mining Data for Nuggets of Knowledge

Knowledge@Wharton, December 10, 1999

When Richard Fairbank, CEO of Capital One, met with Wall Street analysts last month, he told them an unusual story about why his company, a Virginia-based issuer of Visa® and MasterCard®, has been doing well at a time when other credit card issuers are struggling with rising interest rates and ineffective promotions. Recognizing that students represented an undertapped market, Capital One recently delved into new mailing lists and pitched highly targeted offers tailored to students' needs. Result: students, who often dump most credit card offers into dustbins, responded in droves. As Business Week (Nov. 22) points out, Capital One's mailings returned 70% more responses than similar offers to other mailing lists of students.

What was Capital One's secret? The answer lies in a fast-emerging but arcane discipline called data mining, which more and more companies are beginning to employ. As computers have proliferated, most businesses now routinely collect large volumes of data about customers and their transactions. Telecommunications companies and credit card issuers, for example, track phone calls and transactions by millions of customers. Data mining uses sophisticated models drawn from fields ranging from statistics and computer science to artificial intelligence to drill through billions of bits of data for nuggets of information. Ultimately, that information can translate into knowledge and insights about customers and markets.

While companies have long used statistical tools to monitor customer behavior, what sets data mining apart is that it can juggle huge volumes of data, according to Jacob Zahavi, a visiting professor at Wharton. "Conventional statistical methods work well with small data sets," he explains. "Today's databases, however, can involve millions of rows and scores of columns of data."

Zahavi and two colleagues—Lyle Ungar from the University of Pennsylvania's Computer and Information Science department and Robert Stine of Wharton's Statistics department—will teach a short Executive Education course in December about data mining. While industries ranging from financial services to telecommunications have been turning to data mining, the discipline already faces several challenges. One is coping with the coming of the Internet, which has made it easy and inexpensive for companies to collect even larger volumes of data. Another is the strategic challenge that managers face: Who takes ownership of data mining projects in companies where teams from several departments must collaborate to implement them?

Companies like Capital One seem to have answered that question, if the results obtained through their data mining efforts is any indication. Capital One executives analyzed how various classes of customers respond to features ranging from annual fees to interest rates. Then they set varying rates of fees, interest rates and features, developing in all some 7,000 varieties of MasterCard® and Visa® products for different customer groups. Such segmentation allows credit-card companies to manage risk, Zahavi explains. "High-risk customers get offers with high interest rates while those who pay their bills on time get offers with low interest rates," he says. If the data mining model works, it increases the likelihood that customers will receive offers they are most likely to respond to, rather than toss in the garbage can.

Ungar points out that credit-card issuers have also found data mining useful in fraud detection. Companies do this by scanning databases for transactions that don't jell with a customer's past card usage patterns. For instance, a credit card transaction in which a customer, who does not usually do so, buys $2 worth of gasoline immediately raises a red flag, Ungar says, because it might suggest experimental use of a stolen credit card. Credit-card issuers also use data mining to identify customers who represent a high risk of declaring bankruptcy. Telecommunications companies also employ data mining models to track fraudulent phone usage. Long international calls to a country that a user has never called before can signal a stolen phone card or some other kind of abuse.

Pharmaceutical companies often use data mining for both clinical and marketing operations. Stine explains that big drug firms often sort through massive databases of compounds to screen out the most potentially successful ones, a task that is nearly impossible to perform manually. Sometimes, success arrives serendipitously. Pfizer, for example, did not intend to develop Viagra as a treatment for impotence. The drug's original purpose was to relieve angina pain, but data analysis revealed that men who used it experienced sexual arousal, which eventually led to its development as a treatment for impotence.

Despite such successes, data mining also faces major challenges. Zahavi notes that on the technical front, the key hurdle is to develop better algorithms and models that can handle increasingly larger data sets as rapidly as possible. "Scalability is a huge issue in data mining," he notes. "Another technical challenge is developing models that can do a better job analyzing data, detecting nonlinear relationships and interaction between elements."

The key business challenge is identifying problems that can suitably be analyzed with data mining tools. This issue has emerged as a particularly nettlesome one since the explosion of the Internet, as more companies move toward introducing e-commerce. "The rules of customer behavior are different in the Internet environment than they are in the physical world," says Zahavi. "Data are easier to capture on the web, but at the same time customer decision periods are much shorter. Once someone logs onto a certain website, you want to be able to make the right offer to that user during that session.

Special data mining tools may have to be developed to address web-site decisions."

Even if data mining experts figure out ways to deal with the impact of the Internet, a major challenge will still remain. As Stine puts it, at one pharmaceutical company the biggest issues that came up during data mining meetings were organizational rather than statistical. "The database was being designed by the computer sciences group, but the chemistry group was going to collect the data and the statistics group was going to organize it," he says. "So who was responsible for this project? Each group had its own quarterly objectives which didn't necessarily depend on the success of the data mining venture." Stine argues that unless organizations find ways to overcome this kind of silo mentality, it can undermine data mining projects.

For companies that succeed in data mining, however, the rewards can be enormous. "Every company now has more data than ever before about who is using its products and how, and this feedback contains nuggets or patterns," says Stine. "If you could only see those nuggets and recognize those patterns, that could result in a burst of insight." And some bursts of insight can be very profitable. Ask Capital One.

12.

What Does it Take to Lead an E-Commerce Venture?

Knowledge@Wharton, June 7, 2000

Rick Berry, CEO of ICGCommerce.com, often feels he is "driving a Ferrari with a cinderblock on the accelerator." Ask him why, and he will explain that his colleagues and he are slogging around the clock to build an Internet-based procurement business—which should take a decade—and trying to do it in six months. The reason Berry is racing like crazy is simple. "E-procurement is a $10 trillion market worldwide, nearly 30% to 40% of which is not bid—and that is our untapped opportunity," he explains. To grab a chunk of that market before the competition moves in, ICGCommerce.com has set a blistering pace since its launch last October. It already has 350 employees and offices in London and Toronto. Little wonder Berry feels he is speeding down a highway. "You go as fast as you can," he says. "Just don't crash."

Berry is hardly alone. As more and more companies try to seize opportunities in today's volatile Internet environment, they are forced to move at great speed down uncertain—often experimental—paths. This poses enormous leadership challenges for dot-com companies as well as traditional bricks-and-mortar businesses trying to develop e-commerce initiatives. What exactly does it take to lead an e-business effectively in today's fast-changing, technology-driven world? Are traditional leadership skills enough? Or do CEOs and other top executives need to cultivate new capabilities in order to move as fast as possible without crashing?

Answers to these questions and more were discussed at a session on "Transformational Leadership for eCommerce Initiatives" at a meeting of the Wharton Forum on Electronic Commerce on June 1. Moderated by Michael Useem, director of the Wharton Center for Leadership and Change Management, the session involved presentations by Berry, William Kelvie, chief information officer of Fannie Mae, and two MBA students, John Joseph and Kelly Jo Larson. "Leadership is especially important when the future is uncertain," says Useem, who conducted an informal straw poll before the session. He asked: If you were a venture capitalist looking at investing in an enterprise, how much weight would you place on the business model, and how much on the talent of the management team? The response: 50-50. "To succeed in e-commerce, the business model is key, but talent is key as well," says Useem.

Talent must take specific forms to provide effective leadership in e-commerce ventures. According to Berry, the most important quality such leaders must possess is the ability to build a team. Paradoxically, the humility—some might call it egolessness—that is needed to manage a team must go hand-in-hand with the drive and confidence that stems from a strong ego. Leaders of e-commerce ventures must have the ability to attract teams of talented risk-takers. "You have to find people who are willing to put some skin in the game," Berry says. "At ICGCommerce we attracted people who left millions of dollars on the table to join us, and so all of us had a stake in the company."

"Dot-coms typically have a very direct communications style," Berry explains, "and leaders must equip themselves to deal with that." In traditional companies, criticism of a colleague's or subordinate's actions often takes what Berry calls an "oreo cookie" approach—you first say something positive, then slip in your criticism coupled with a suggested change, and end by saying something positive again. The fast-paced e-commerce world, however, simply doesn't permit the luxury of such a leisurely approach. "You communicate directly, and you must build a team that can cope with that," he says.

The speed at which everyone works in an e-commerce venture also means little time is available to train anyone. "Your team members must come with a set of skills and deliver," says Berry. "You need people with lots of experience who know how things are done, and go out and do them." A corollary, he adds, is that team members must have confidence bordering on arrogance. In addition, they must have enormous amounts of energy and stamina—because the environment often requires 18-hour days and weekends that blur into the work week.

Leaders of e-commerce ventures must strive to create a specific type of work culture, Berry notes. This culture is high-energy and result-oriented. It doesn't allow time for studies or leisurely thought-processes. It fosters decision-making based on incomplete information. "We have an aggressive culture," Berry says. "We always ask ourselves, 'So what?' And we have a culture that is highly solution-oriented. If you have a problem, you've got to come up with at least three solutions."

While the work culture must emphasize hard work, it must also be fun. "People love to win," he adds. Among other things, the work culture must be athletic and competitive. It must be driven by people who hate to lose, who will fight every battle to the end, and who will be prepared to die for the cause." They must also be driven by a sense of urgency. "There's a time window within which we can do something, and it is closing," says Berry.

Another crucial capability of Internet leaders, Berry notes, is that they must be constantly upbeat and uplifting. "It is like being on stage all day long," he says. "Your work has to be a constant euphoric event." ICGCommerce uses a method to sustain the euphoria. Everybody in the company regularly gets an e-mail about "Five Great Things that Happened Today."

Other panelists agreed with Berry. Fannie Mae's Kelvie points out that leaders of e-commerce ventures must be visionary—in addition to being as tenacious as shelty dogs. He adds that a vital aspect of leadership in e-commerce ventures involves the ability to attract and retain talented staff. "I used to draw upon talent in other companies, and now I'm getting raided," he says. "I live every day with the war for talent."

Joseph and Larson, who have been working with Useem on a website about leadership in the Internet age, based their presentations on interview with leaders of e-commerce companies as well as those in traditional companies. Quoting David Perry, founder of Chemdex, a B2B site for the life sciences industry, Joseph says that leadership often entails developing a virtuous circle of "raising money, so you can hire good people, so you can make and sell good products, so you can raise more money." He adds that other leaders of e-commerce ventures emphasized the importance of nurturing a strong culture, which begins with hiring the right kind of people—who are enthusiastic, passionate, and share the organization's values.

Larson points out that the speed at which the Internet world moves has often made it difficult for traditional companies to compete effectively with dot-com companies. The reason is that leaders of dot-coms often do things "that are probably correct—or correct directionally—but may also turn out to be wrong." This requires a mindset in which the organization views failure as the tuition for success. Traditional bricks-and-mortar companies, however, are not built to tolerate failure. "You need leaders who are willing to be taught as they lead," she says.

13.

"Venture Capital Has Gone From One Unreality to Another"

Knowledge@Wharton, January TK, 2002

On January 9 the Barksdale Group, a high-profile $180 million venture fund launched by former Netscape CEO Jim Barksdale and his partners, quietly announced that it was closing shop. It is a sign of the times. If one industry has been severely mauled following the twin dot-com and telecom debacles, that industry is venture capital—or private equity, as it is sometimes called. During the late 1990s venture capitalists—lured by sky-high valuations for high-tech start-ups of every ilk—poured millions of dollars into enterprises that have now gone down in flames. And with the fate of a broader economic turnaround still uncertain, it might be a while before the prospects of venture capitalists improve.

So what lies ahead for venture capital? Continuing its series of conversations with senior executives, Knowledge@Wharton spoke to William P. Egan II, a founder and managing general partner of Boston-based Alta Communications—which has some $1 billion under management. In 1979 he also founded its predecessor firm, Burr, Egan, Deleage & Co. Egan's introduction to the world of private equity came soon after he graduated from Wharton and became a manager of venture capital for New England Enterprise Capital Associates. He is a former president and chairman of the National Venture Capital Association.

Knowledge@Wharton: When did the slowdown hit the private equity business? Did the terrorist attacks of September 11 have a major impact?

Egan: The private equity business was starting to slow down pretty dramatically from the middle of 2000; Sept. 11 just put an exclamation point on that slowdown. For example, we have a Monday morning meeting in our firm every other week. In 1999 we would have had five pages of transactions that we would be interested in doing. That was the amount of deal activity. But during 2001, that went down to a page and a half. I speak now not about the quality but the quantity of deals. Also, I was speaking recently to one of our limited partners and learned that the investors were experiencing a mild percentage of capital drawn against commitments. That was running, up until this year, at about 40% at this large retirement fund, which would suggest about a two-and-a-half year investment cycle. At the quarter ended June 2001, he reported to me that they were running at about 12%. This would suggest about an eight-year investment cycle. Obviously the pace will pick up, but it gives you a sense of how dramatically the train has slowed.

Knowledge@Wharton: What brought this about?

Egan: From my perspective, we went through two significant phenomena. First, there was the Internet phenomenon; and second, we saw the telecommunications sector go through boom and bust cycles. Both areas saw unprecedented investment activity. Particularly in telecom there was an if-you-build-it-they-will-come sort of mentality. We have gone from that to a huge swing to the other end of the spectrum. Now the only thing that people want to look at are fully-funded business plans. In other words, we've gone from a market where people were building new networks—no matter what the cost—in the hope that they would find the business to support it, to a different environment where you have to prove that whatever you build, you have enough capital to complete that. We have gone from one unreality to another. It's like a bell-shaped curve. We have figured out the lunatic fringe of each side. Now I hope good judgment will come into play and we will move back toward the middle.

Knowledge@Wharton: Do you see any middle ground emerging?

Egan: Oh yes. I've been in this business since 1970. At our annual meeting a year ago, we were showing very good numbers in one of our funds. They were not good enough to put us into the top quartile at that time, but today they would certainly be considered astronomical. I remember saying to one of our limited partners at that meeting, "Whatever we do today, I want you to leave with one memory. And that is, 'This too will pass.'" In other words, things were way too good. They were unsustainably good.

Knowledge@Wharton: What's happening now?

Egan: We are now in normal financial markets, in my mind, over a 30-year period. When a pendulum swings to excess, nature requires that it swing back. For instance in the Internet area, there will have to be some companies succeeding, and there are. We also continue to believe that in the long term there will be numerous significant opportunities in telecommunications. In fact, there are several companies, both public and private, that are going to be successful businesses, but they will have to be financially restructured to get them on the right footing. That is one of the reasons why things are going to be slower coming back in the telecom area for venture capital or private equity. It will take some time for the problems to get sorted through.

Knowledge@Wharton: Can you explain how you see the telecom market turning around?

Egan: Numerous companies, both public and private, have significant revenues and earning capacity, but they are too highly leveraged. In a nutshell, the people who own that high-yield debt are going to have to become shareholders. The existing shareholders are going to have to be squeezed down—but once you do that, you have a very interesting business proposition. You have companies that have tens of millions of dollars in EBITDA (earnings before interest, taxes and depreciation), but far too much debt to support that level of earnings. But if you restructure that debt so that it becomes equity, those businesses are not just okay, they are very attractive. There are several of these companies, and they are not hard to come by. They have substantial high-yield debt and are trading at substantial discounts. A very good case can be made that until these companies restructure it is going to be very difficult to do any further financing.

Knowledge@Wharton: What went wrong at these companies?

Egan: These companies got into debt for one of two reasons. They either built too much capacity, or they funded too many losses.

If all this had been done with equity, the companies may not have had good equity returns, but they would still have had cash flow. They got all this capital because money was fungible. At the end of the boom cycle, money had no value. The idea was worth so much more than capital. Frankly, ideas tended to be worth more even than management. That is why you ended up with so many companies that could not succeed being funded. These companies had neither good management nor the function that good management performs—a thoughtful use of capital. So all you ended up with was a bunch of ideas. And most of us in the private equity business were part of this folly.

This is not unusual. The same kind of phenomenon went on in the early 1980s when there was a biotech bubble. The difference this time was the unprecedented size of the private equity business and the scale at which things were done. But you can go back and see the same kind of mentality in biotech, or when Lotus 123 was developed and everyone was saying there would be 10,000 successful shrink-wrapped software companies. There have always been these periodic waves of euphoria. It's what Greenspan called "irrational exuberance," but in a curious way, that is probably what makes capitalism work. There's a new wunderkind—or ten of them—on the cover of some magazine, and that gets everyone excited about the prospects. In my opinion, there's no question that the Internet/telecom bubble was a mania. I am an optimist, but I think the downturns make the private equity business stronger. You learn more with your failures than you ever do with your successes. Your losses can be the best base from which to create new successes.

Knowledge@Wharton: In this environment, do you see any reasons why investors should remain in the private equity business?

Egan: Private equity investing has been a very attractive area for institutions because it is a business where the investor group has an unfair advantage—in the sense that it is not an auction market. I often tell my associates that the day an entrepreneur can go to a machine and ask for bids for his offering, that's when I don't want to be in this business. In private equity the real value is that you help entrepreneurs. But from an investment standpoint, you also have the ability to be the market maker in a security and the buyer of that security. It's a wonderful business. Results in the 1999-2000 time frame have been very tough, but it is not the first time this business has seen tough results. If you look at it over a long period, it has been a very beneficial period. If you are in the right time or place, you still have the chance to make a lot of money.

I have been in this business for a long time. The right time to make an investment in an early stage investment is during a downturn. One reason for that is that capital tends to be valued higher so you can get a better deal as an investor. Second, people resources are far more available. A lot of good people are looking for work. And third, in a startup you are not going to get many sales, so in a downturn you don't care that there aren't many orders coming around. So you focus on developing opportunities that will surface two or three years from now. That is why a down cycle is a good time to be doing this.

Knowledge@Wharton: Where do you see opportunities today?

Egan: We run a fairly specialized fund. We do traditional media— radio, televison, etc.—and telecommunications and then some Internet infrastructure kind of activity. We continue to think that the traditional media businesses will be enormously steady. Telecom wireless activity is going to be significant in the U.S.

and overseas. There's a range of opportunities in that world. With what we have gone through, there will be fewer players competing for those activities. But everyone in the private equity business will have to reevaluate their approach toward businesses that require enormous amounts of capital. In telecommunications, particularly, the opportunities going forward will have to be more capital efficient.

Knowledge@Wharton: What is the most important lesson you have learned from the dot-com and telecom bombs?

Egan: I have often heard it said in the private equity business that people are very important. I have come to the conclusion after 30 years in this business that management talent is a necessary but not sufficient reason to succeed. Management can never be overvalued, but it can be overestimated. Warren Buffett once said, show me a bad business and a good management and the bad business will prevail every time. So the lesson I have learned from the recent mania is that you may have capital and a talented management team, but if you are fundamentally in a lousy business, you won't get the kind of results you would in a good business. All businesses aren't created equal.

14.

"We Are All Bound to One Another at the Hip"

Knowledge@Wharton, June 7, 2000

The emergence of the Internet has changed many things about business. One thing that hasn't changed, however, is that building a lasting, values-based company takes leaders who passionately believe in their vision—and are willing to change themselves to achieve it. David S. Pottruck, co-CEO of Charles Schwab, and

Terry Pearce, a teacher at the University of California in Berkeley and a communications officer at Schwab, explore these themes in their new book, *Clicks and Mortar: Passion Driven Growth in an Internet Driven World*. Reviewing the book for The New York Times, Fred Andrews wrote: "If there is a better handbook on adapting to the Internet economy, I have yet to find it." Pearce discussed the key themes of the book in a recent conversation with Knowledge@Wharton.

Knowledge@Wharton: How did you come to write this book?

Pearce: In 1992 Dave Pottruck was searching for a consultant who could look over some of his speeches and articles, and I worked with him to see what we could do to publish them. We soon made an amazing connection and became close friends. I have a background in teaching and in business—I spent 16 years in IBM—and have always been very interested in leadership. I started introducing Dave to some leadership theory, and frankly, we were both single at that time so we spent a lot of time together talking about theory. He was clearly on the fast track at Schwab, and Dave felt that he had a long way to grow. Over the next several years we not only developed theory, but we were also able to put it into practice.

It became clear that what kept Schwab in the lead was the fact that it had the ability to change rapidly—almost to reinvent itself. That pace accelerated because of the Internet. We put together a lot of conversations on what actually had to happen. Since Dave is a marvelous speaker, we had a chance to document these changes as they were happening through his speeches, through my own writing, and through some articles that we worked on together. In 1995 Schwab documented its vision, and right after that we started talking about writing this book. The more we discussed it, the more we realized that the book could become a legacy for Schwab's leadership as the company was reinventing itself.

The interesting sidelight was that we became very good friends at the same time and realized very early on that in order to change the company, you had to change yourself. You could not change the organization unless you had first drunk the water yourself. You had to go through internal changes.

Knowledge@Wharton: What do you mean by "drinking the water yourself?"

Pearce: My earlier studies in leadership and communication dealt with people who saw things that others did not see—and who worked to make their vision a reality. But in today's world, a leader must be authentic in order to inspire people. And inspiration, I believe, is the coin of the realm. It is no longer possible to lead a company in this environment by telling people what to do. Leadership has become much more private and personal—and yet, much more public at the same time. Leadership doesn't begin with emotion any more; it begins with personal decisions. You have to know what your values are, and what is important to you, in order to inspire people. That was not always the case. In the past you did things to get 2% more of market share or to drive 10 more automobiles off the plant floor. But today you must inspire people with the values you hold. Unless you have gone through internal changes yourself, you cannot inspire people.

There's a great story about Gandhi. A woman brought her young son to him and said, "Would you talk to him? He eats too much sugar." Gandhi asked her to bring him back in two weeks. She brought her son back two weeks later, and Gandhi spoke very eloquently about why the boy should stop eating too much sugar. The mother told Gandhi, "That was very effective. But why did you ask me to bring him back in two weeks?" Gandhi said, "I first had to stop eating sugar myself." He knew that he could not express his argument authentically unless he first went through that change himself.

The same principle now applies to business. With the coming of the Internet, people know everything, and that creates a fertile ground for cynicism. If you are authentic, you have a tremendous advantage over someone who is trying to manipulate or hide things. Such people will eventually be found out, and that adds to the cynicism. But authenticity breeds productivity. That's the corollary. The more excited and passionate you are about what you are doing, the more your enthusiasm will catch on.

Knowledge@Wharton: In your book you tell a story about Tom Seip, an executive who was passed up for the president's job at Schwab. Could you please summarize that story, and comment on what it means to build such values into a company's culture?

Pearce: Tom Seip had been a headhunter, and he actually recruited Dave for Schwab. He was then asked to come in and take over as head of HR. He was very smart and rose very rapidly, but in 1997 there were several changes in the upper structure of management at Schwab. Tom was considered for the president's job, but there was another person, who had been with the company for less time than Tom, and he was very, very smart. Dave and Charles Schwab and others felt that this other person was better qualified than Tom to become the company president, and so they passed Tom over.

This was a very difficult decision, because they had all been friends, and Tom, frankly, took it very hard. But there is something about executives who get that far in building a values-based company, that they are very self-aware. Tom was introspective enough to know exactly what was going on. He first said that he would leave, and then he said he would reconsider.

Finally he wrote to the Schwab senior management team after being passed over for the biggest promotion of his career, and he said, "Leaving would be the worst thing I could do. It would be contrary to everything I believe in, and I would be sorry in 15 days.... The only reason for me to leave would be petulance, because I did not get to play the position I wanted.... I asked myself, 'How am I going to explain this to Jake, my 12-year-old son, that I left because I didn't get to be starting center forward? I had no answer to that...and I couldn't find one. It's nice to go to work every day feeling like you are doing something important...fundamentally to help people...and doing it with people you care about. It doesn't get a whole lot better than that." And he stayed.

Let me now address the question about how you build that kind of culture. At Schwab, it started with the individual. Charles Schwab, the entrepreneur, was a person with those values. So it was not as though a bunch of people who came in said they had to change the culture. That was always the case. Where Charles Schwab Co. was smart was in recognizing what the company had. It saw that its values-based culture—a part of its DNA—was a fundamental competitive strength, and it spent a lot of time building and sustaining this culture. That is what companies have to do. This is particularly important in a company where you can have people coming from organizations with different cultures.

Knowledge@Wharton: Which companies, other than Schwab, have done a good job building a values-based culture?

Pearce: There aren't too many such companies. Most of them have the founders' stamp on them still. One of them that comes to mind right away is Hewlett-Packard. Apple is another good example.

Knowledge@Wharton: When companies merge, you sometimes have a situation where two CEOs have to share power. This is often difficult. And yet, at a time when organizations are becoming so complex that no individual has all the skills needed to manage them, how can executives learn to share power while still exercising leadership?

Pearce: If I had the answer, I would be out sailing somewhere. But we have some great examples. It seems to me that leaders have to understand the difficulty of putting the cultures of their organizations together. That goes beyond just the financial engineering of the merger. So how can CEOs work together? Nothing drives the ego like failure. If executives refuse to share power, there will be enough failure to make even the biggest of egos think again.

The entrepreneur who builds his company into something big has to gravitate to becoming a flag-carrier for the company and has to delegate operational jobs to others. A couple of things happen when the leader does that. First, the quality of the operations improves, because one person cannot do it all. And second, it gives people the message that they have power, and they can be effective. When you do that, you not only spread the company's financial wealth but also its psychic wealth. Spreading psychic wealth is one of the most important qualities of a leader. Leaders who don't do that tend to fail.

Knowledge@Wharton: How should leaders manage the trade-off between meeting short-term goals and long-term goals? When a company is busy planning how to meet its quarterly performance targets, isn't there a real danger that long-term goals will be pushed aside? What advice do you have for executives who have to navigate through such situations?

Pearce: Well, I have this advice: Any time you make a choice between doing this or that, you have to do things that are important in the short-term or in the long-term. The secret really is to do both.

You cannot disregard the fact that the company's first obligation is to stay in business, so you must do the things that keep the company going. But even in the midst of what appears to be greed on Wall Street, there is also a counter-force. The wealthiest people are recognizing more and more that joy in life comes from serving others. Money is part of the game—and a necessary part of the game—but the key to keeping your customers loyal lies in serving them well over the lifetime of their relationship with you. So the two things should go together. When they do not, you have a problem. When any CEO loses this perspective, he or she is bound to fall into difficulties.

I often remind my students that society is older than business. Business has grown over the years into a very complex phenomenon, but we should not forget that society began with human beings sharing and serving one another. In that sense, sharing and service are fundamental to our existence. We sometimes lose sight of that fact because of all the complexity of business. We are all bound to one another at the hip.

Knowledge@Wharton: How can passion be sustained? It may be easy to be passionate in a start-up, but as a company grows large and routines set in, it tends to lose its entrepreneurial fervor. How should executives deal with that?

Pearce: I think about this a lot. When you get together with someone and say, "Let's do something great together," it feels wonderful. It gets your juices flowing—you have the excitement of setting goals together, seeing what can be done, and it's fun. It also has an impact. The end point is to go and do something else together. That's the way to keep the excitement alive, by doing things together. When people build something together—something great that will not just be remembered in the future, but will also make a mark on society and establish a legacy, they can keep their entrepreneurial spirit alive.

You've got to remember two things. One is the excitement of doing something well with your team. The other is the matter of making a difference, leaving a legacy and giving something back to posterity. That is why you've got to make sure that the leaders of the organization are focused on inspiring passion, and maintaining and building a culture in which people are excited about what they are doing. Unless they do that, people will stop reinventing themselves. You've got to constantly emphasize to the company as a whole, "Don't forget what really matters." You sustain this culture through stories that are told and re-told not just once in 10 years but once in a year or even once in six months. You must do this throughout your organization, over and over again. That's what it takes to become and remain passion-driven.

ENDNOTES

Introduction

1 "Goals, Values and Performance," Contemporary Strategy Analysis, Robert M. Grant. Third edition 1998.
2 "eBay: Last Man Standing," *Knowledge@Wharton*, April 10, 2002.

Chapter 1

1 "Can You Sell Groceries Like Books?" *Business Week*, July 26, 1999.
2 "Webvan To Sell Technology; Automated System Gets $2.5 Million Bid by Borders Arm," *San Jose Mercury News*, September 22, 2001.
3 "Tesco Bets Small—And Wins Big," *Business Week*, October 1, 2001.
4 Tesco.com press release issued June 25, 2001.
5 Interview with author in August 2001.
6 "Co-Founder of Borders to Launch Online Megagrocer," *The Wall Street Journal*, April 22, 1999.
7 *The Wall Street Journal*, April 22, 1999.
8 Webvan press release on Business Wire, June 2, 1999.
9 Figures quoted in "Venture Capital Industry: Refreshed and Ready to Rebound?" *Knowledge@Wharton*, August 30, 2000.

10 "An Ambitious Internet Grocer Is Out of Both Cash and Ideas," *The New York Times*, July 10, 2001.

11 *Business Week*, October 1, 2001.

12 Selected financial consolidated data provided in form 10-K filed with the Securities and Exchange Commission for the year ended December 31, 2000.

13 Corporate information taken from the Tesco.com Web site.

14 "Tesco Bets Small—And Wins Big," *Business Week*, October 1, 2001.

15 Tesco.com announcement, June 25, 2001.

16 Author interview.

Chapter 2

1   "Year-end Shutdowns Report: Shutdowns More Than Doubled in 2001," Webmergers.com, December 2001.

2   "The Impact of Internet and Electronic Technologies on Firms and Its Implications for Competitive Advantage," by Harbir Singh, Sendil Ethiraj and Isin Guler. Working Paper, Department of Management, Wharton School.

3   Subscription information appears on the www.brittannica.com Web site.

4   "Britannica.com Cuts United States Staff, Adds Fees," CNET News.com, March 13, 2001.

5   "eBay: Last Man Standing," *Knowledge@Wharton*, April 10, 2002.

6   Wit Capital's acquisition of E*Offering.com was reported in *E-Commerce Times*, May 15, 2000.

7   The Impact of Internet and Electronic Technologies on Firms and Its Implications for Competitive Advantage," by Harbir Singh, Sendil Ethiraj and Isin Guler. Working Paper, Department of Management, Wharton School.

8   "Dot-com Era Notions Guided a Huge Merger," *The New York Times*, July 19, 2002.

9   "Value Drivers of E-Commerce Business Models," Working Paper, Wharton E-Business Initiative.

10 *The Guardian*, May 8, 2001.

11 "Second Sight," *The Guardian*, September 27, 2001.

12 "Web Currency Results in Hill of Beans," *St. Louis Post-Dispatch*, August 29, 2001.

13 "Carlson Marketing Group purchases Beenz.com," press release on www.cmg.carlson.com.

Chapter 3

1   "Economy, the Web and E-Commerce: Amazon.com," an online chat with CEO Jeff Bezos on December 6, 2001.
2   The rest of this chapter is based on an article about customer behavior and e-commerce strategy that appeared in the Financial Times Mastering Management series on November 13, 2000. The article was written by Eric Clemons and Michael Row.

Chapter 4

1   Eric Clemons examines these issues in a paper titled "E-Commerce Risks."
2   "Strategic Alliances Need not End Up in Divorce Court," *Knowledge@Wharton*, October 12, 1999. This section is based on that article.
3   The authors are Harbir Singh and Prashant Kale.
4   "Priceline and Expedia Bury the Ax," *Business Week*, January 22, 2001.
5   Eric K. Clemons and Lorin M. Hitt, professors of Operations and Information Management at Wharton, address this issue in a paper titled, "Poaching and the Loss of Intellectual Property: An Increasingly Important Form of Opportunism."
6   Reports about the latest phase of the Intel-AMD price rivalry have appeared in several business publications, including *The San Jose Mercury News*, October 18, 2001.

Chapter 5

1   "Surviving the E-Trading Explosion," *Knowledge@Wharton*, June 9, 1999.
2   Ameritrade 10Q filed with the Securities and Exchange Commission, referring to the quarter ended December 31, 2001.
3   "Sale of Datek Online Set for Early Next Week," *Financial Times*, March 19, 2002.
4   "Online brokerages diversify and hope for rebound," *Financial Times*, December 24, 2001.
5   E*Trade press release issued on February 13, 2002.
6   "Changing Channel Distribution Models in the Internet Age," *Knowledge@Wharton*, June 6, 2001.
7   "Surviving the E-Trading Explosion," *Knowledge@Wharton*, June 8, 1999.

8 "In a Slump, Charles Schwab and Merrill Lynch Seek Middle Ground," *Knowledge@Wharton*, July 18, 2001.

9 "There's Still a Lot of Life Left in These Old Economy Companies," *Knowledge@Wharton*, February 22, 2001.

10 Company press release issued on January 15, 2002.

11 "Scratching the Surface: Capital One Revolutionizes Credit Card Marketing," *The Washington Post*, October 30, 2000.

12 Capital One press release, January 15, 2002.

13 "Capital One: Exploiting an Information-Based Strategy," case study by Eric K. Clemons and Matt E. Thatcher.

14 "Leaders Who Get It," *Darwin Magazine*, October 2001.

15 "Capital One: Exploiting an Information-Based Strategy," case study by Eric K. Clemons and Matt E. Thatcher.

16 "Capital One: Exploiting an Information-Based Strategy," case study by Eric K. Clemons and Matt E. Thatcher.

17 Quoted in "Capital One: Exploiting an Information-Based Strategy," case study by Eric K. Clemons and Matt E. Thatcher.

18 "Scratching the Surface: Capital One Revolutionizes Credit Card Marketing," *The Washington Post*, October 30, 2000.

19 "Scratching the Surface," *The Washington Post*, October 30, 2000.

20 "Scratching the Surface," *The Washington Post*, October 30, 2000.

21 "Charging into Europe," *CIO*, November 1, 2000.

22 "Taking Credit: Balance-Sheet Sleuths Look for Snares in a Post-Enron World," *Barrons*, February 9, 2002.

Chapter 6

1 "Dotcom Bomb Hits the Publications that Covered it," *Knowledge@Wharton*, August 29, 2001.

2 "The Street news site announces cutbacks; British operations are closed down," *The Washington Post*, November 17, 2000.

3 Howard Kurtz, "The Fortune Tellers: Inside Wall Street's Game of Money, Media and Manipulation," published in June 2001.

4 "Is Online Journalism on the way out? Websites struggle financially despite millions of visitors," *The Washington Post*, February 21, 2001.

5 Reported by Reuters, August 16, 2000.

6   "TheStreet.com's Slippery Slope: Once High-Flying Financial News Site Struggles for Survival," *The San Francisco Chronicle*, November 2, 2000.
7   TheStreet.com reported this figure to the Securities and Exchange Commission on its Form 10Q filed on November 14, 2001.
8   TheStreet.com, form 10Q filed with the SEC on November 14, 2001.
9   "James J. Cramer finds Truth and Inspiration in the Shopping Habits of Americans," *Knowledge@Wharton*.
10 "How the Recession Has Changed the Advertising and Marketing Industries," *Knowledge@Wharton*, December 19, 2001. All of Weisenburger's remarks appeared in this article.
11 Quoted in "Will Consumers Be Willing to Pay for Their Formerly Free Content on the Internet?" *Knowledge@Wharton*, August 29, 2001.
12 "Will Consumers Be Willing to Pay for Their Formerly Free Content on the Internet?" *Knowledge@Wharton*, August 29, 2001.
13 "Gray Lady Green," *Forbes*, November 30, 2001.
14 "Gray Lady Green," *Forbes*, November 30, 2001.

Chapter 7

1   "A Hit to the Mail is a Hit to the Economy," *Business Week*, November 19, 2001.
2   "Anthrax prompts shift in Fed's e-mail policy," *ComputerWorld* report published on CNN.com on October 30, 2001.
3   "Hallmark.com can't greet all online visitors," CNET News.com, December 21, 2001.
4   AOL Time Warner reported AOL subscription numbers in a press release dated October 17, 2001. AOL added 6.7 million new subscribers during the past year.
5   Stamps.com announced its acquisition of E-Stamp's name, patents and other intellectual property in a press release on April 30, 2001. The release added that "the portfolio of 31 patents and trademarks largely relate to Internet-based postage printing and management."
6   *Knowledge@Wharton*, December 10, 1999. Kapoor was one of several dot-com entrepreneurs to speak at the Wharton India Economic Forum that year.
7   E-Stamp described its market opportunity in its registration statement filed with the Securities and Exchange Commission when the company went public in 1999.

8 Grant's analysis appeared in the Gartner Viewpoint column on CNET News.com on November 27, 2000.

9 Stamps.com, 10-Q statement filed with the Securities and Exchange Commission on November 14, 2001.

10 "Stamps.com adds shipping, mailing with iShip buy," *Bloomberg News,* October 25, 1999.

11 Stamps.com explained this in its form 10-K document filed with the SEC in April 2001.

12 Stamps.com, 10-K document, filed in April 2001.

13 Stamps.com made this disclosure in Form 10-Q filed with the Securities and Exchange Commission on November 14, 2001.

14 "Stamps.com sticks to price increase," CNET News.com, June 21, 2001.

Chapter 8

1 "Opportunities for B2B e-Commerce in Real Estate," *Knowledge@Wharton,* November 22, 2000.

2 "Commerce One Shifts to Old Territory," CNET News.com, January 22, 2002.

3 "The Evolution of B2B: Lessons from the Auto Industry," *Knowledge@Wharton,* November 21, 2001.

4 "VerticalNet Bets on the B2B Market," *Knowledge@Wharton,* January 20, 2000.

5 "VerticalNet: Survivor or Another Dot-Com Disaster," *Knowledge@Wharton,* December 6, 2000.

6 *Business Week* Online, March 26, 2002.

7 Covisint history as it appears on the company's Web site.

8 "Will Covisint Thrive as a B2B Exchange," *Knowledge@Wharton,* April 25, 2001.

9 *Detroit Free Press,* February 9, 2002.

Index

219